The Northeast
1. Freedom Trail
2. Harvard University
3. Plymouth Rock
4. Niagara Falls
5. Hyde Park
6. West Point Military Academy
7. Statue of Liberty
8. Manhattan
9. The Metropolitan Museum
10. Atlantic City
11. Independence Park
12. Fallingwater
13. Gettysburg National Military Park
14. Ft. McHenry National Monument
15. Inner Harbor

The Southeast
16. Washington, D.C.
17. The Smithsonian Institution
18. Arlington National Cemetery
19. Mt. Vernon
20. Monticello
21. Colonial Williamsburg
22. Busch Gardens, The Old Country
23. Churchill Downs
24. Graceland
25. The Grand Old Opry/Opryland
26. The Biltmore Estate
27. Stone Mountain
28. Walt Disney World
29. Busch Gardens, The Dark Continent
30. Everglades National Park
31. John F. Kennedy Space Center

The Central Region
32. Chicago
33. The Museum of Science & Industry
34. The Art Institute of Chicago
35. Lincoln's Home & Tomb
36. The Gateway Arch
37. The Truman Home & Library
38. Mark Twain Home & Museum
39. The Henry Ford Museum & Greenfield Village
40. The French Quarter
41. Gilley's Club
42. The Astrodome
43. Six Flags Over Texas
44. The Alamo
45. Mount Rushmore

The West
46. Yellowstone National Park
47. The Mormon Tabernacle
48. Las Vegas
49. Hoover Dam
50. Monument Valley
51. London Bridge
52. Carlsbad Caverns
53. The Grand Canyon
54. The Painted Desert/ The Petrified Forest
55. The San Diego Zoo
56. Sea World
57. The Queen Mary/ The Spruce Goose
58. Disneyland
59. Los Angeles
60. Universal Studios Hollywood
61. Los Angeles County Museum of Art
62. Yosemite National Park
63. San Simeon State Historical Monument
64. San Francisco
65. The Space Needle

American Landmarks
AND POPULAR PLACES

American

Landmarks

AND POPULAR PLACES

SYLVIA WEBB

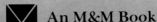

MALLARD PRESS

An Imprint of BDD Promotional Book Company, Inc.
666 Fifth Avenue, New York, N.Y. 10103

An M&M Book

(Previous pages) Rising from the fabled fog of San Francisco Bay is perhaps the most beautiful bridge in the world — the Golden Gate.

An Imprint of BDD Promotional
Book Company, Inc.
666 Fifth Avenue
New York, N.Y. 10103

First published in the United States of
America in 1989 by The Mallard Press.

ISBN 0 792 45114-7 1998

American Landmarks and Popular Places
was prepared and produced by
Moore & Moore Publishing,
11 W. 19th Street, New York, N.Y. 10011

An M & M Book

Project Director & Editor Gary Fishgall

Photo Research Deborah Robbins,
Grace Sullivan, Jana Marcus

Senior Editorial Assistant Shirley
Vierheller; **Editorial Assistants** Lisa
Pike, Ben McLaughlin, Mitchell Weisberg

Designer Binns & Lubin/Martin Lubin

Separations and Printing Tien Wah
Press (PTE) Ltd., Singapore

Typesetting Sharon Brant Typography

CONTENTS

INTRODUCTION

This is a celebration of place, a pictorial odyssey to nearly 100 of the best-loved and most-visited locations in the United States. Their enduring appeal is both obvious and subtle. Some are destinations of unsurpassed natural beauty; others represent superb engineering achievements with intrinsic beauty of their own. Some possess innate historical significance; others help us understand the individuals who helped make that history. Some educate us; others amuse us. All are elements of the mosaic that is America.

We celebrate the nation's beauty in the mighty cascade of Niagara Falls and the nearly imperceptible flow of the Everglades, in the steaming fountains of Yellowstone Park and the arid magnificence of Monument Valley, in the brilliant clarity of the Painted Desert and the underground monoliths of Carlsbad Caverns. In such places we see the hand of nature shaping the land and leaving in its wake awesome majesty. We come from them uplifted that we are a part of such beauty and humbled that we are such a small part.

We admire the nation's ingenuity, marveling at those who carved Mount Rushmore, built Hoover Dam, erected Sears Tower, and assembled Apollo rockets. Their daring is breathtaking especially when the underlying goals are considered: rendering mammoth likenesses of four presidents from the unforgiving face of a rock wall; taming the nation's most dangerous river and channeling its turbulent waters for irrigation and recreation; piercing the clouds with the world's tallest building; defying gravity and putting men on the moon. In these accomplishments we see the hands of men and women shaping the forces of nature and their efforts are a testament to the ongoing vitality of the country's pioneering spirit.

We witness that spirit anew as we trace the nation's history—from the granite rock at Plymouth, Massachusetts, where the Pilgrims landed some 370 years ago, to the marble memorial at Washington, D.C., commemorating the fallen of the Vietnam War just a generation ago. We seek clues to that spirit in the public monuments but also in the private homes of those who helped forge and guide the country. In Washington's Mount Vernon, Jefferson's Monticello, Lincoln's Springfield, Roosevelt's Hyde Park, and Truman's Independence, there are beginnings and endings, each a chapter in the national book. Their stories become ours, as these places give reality to the American people's dreams, struggles, and ultimate triumphs or tragedies.

We seek to satisfy our curiosity about a myriad other things as we explore our great museums, delving into the world's treasures—from the arts of antiquity to the sciences of today. We see a Pleistocene fossil of an animal that once swam in a long-gone inland sea, an Egyptian temple that stood along the Nile, a German submarine that prowled beneath the North Atlantic, an American spacecraft that hurtled around the moon— and we find that our understanding has been enlarged.

Then, sometimes, we indulge ourselves in just plain fun. Ever fascinated by celebrities, we visit the estates of the rich and the famous. Ever intrigued by fantasy, we are drawn to the bright lights of Broadway and Hollywood. Ever optimistic, we may try our luck in the casinos of Las Vegas and Atlantic City. Ever adventurous, we flock to theme parks to be whirled and twirled, thrilled and spilled, rattled and rolled in a marvelous menagerie of mechanical contraptions that robustly express America's still-youthful exuberance.

All of these places allow us to better understand the past, savor the present, glimpse the future. Their appeal is enduring, for it lies in us.

(Opposite) "We have no national temples but the Capitol," said 19th-century Congressman Rufas Choate of this inspiring building whose first small wing was completed in 1800.

The Northeast

The Freedom Trail

Running through the heart of downtown Boston, amid the highrise office buildings, shops, and restaurants, the three-mile Freedom Trail passes through some of the most historic real estate in the United States—16 structures and sites that bear witness to America's struggle for independence. Beginning at Boston Common, where British troops mustered before the Battle of Bunker Hill in 1775, the thick red line of demarcation wends its way across the mouth of Boston Harbor to Charlestown and to Bunker Hill itself. Along the way, it passes such landmarks of American history as the home of Paul Revere and the Old North Church, which was used to hang the lanterns that told Revere of the British route ("one if by land, two if by sea"). Other sights include the Old State House, seat of the colonial government;

a ring of cobblestones designating the site of the Boston Massacre; the Old South Meeting House, where the "Sons of Liberty" planned the Boston Tea Party; and Faneuil Hall, known as the "Cradle of Liberty" for the protest meetings it housed.

On Bunker Hill, a 220-foot obelisk marks the site of one of the major battles of the Revolution, and below, in the Charlestown Navy Yard, is a relic of yet another war between the British and her former colonists, the War of 1812. That, of course, is the U.S.S. *Constitution,* "Old Ironsides," undefeated in several major engagements and the world's oldest commissioned warship still afloat.

(Left) A highlight along the 16-site route is a visit to the U.S.S. *Constitution,* "Old Ironsides," berthed in the Charlestown Navy Yard.

(Previous pages) The Statue of Liberty points the way toward lower Manhattan, where, on the left, stand the twin towers of the World Trade Center.

In Paul Revere Mall, adjacent to "Old North Church," the famed patriot perpetually rides in a sculpture by Cyrus E. Dallin.

The dual symbols of the British Empire, the Lion, shown here, and the Unicorn gaze out on modern Boston from atop the Old State House, seat of the colonial government.

Bunker Hill Monument commemorates one of the earliest Revolutionary War battles which is reenacted in a multimedia show at the Pavilion next door.

(Opposite) In recent years, Faneuil Hall, the "Cradle of Liberty," has been reborn as a marketplace teaming with food stands, crafts stalls, boutiques, and restaurants.

The Harvard University campus offers an intriguing mixture of architectural styles, from stately Georgian buildings on the Yard to James Stirling's postmodern Sackler Museum a few blocks away.

Harvard University

Founded in 1636, Harvard University is one of the oldest and most prestigious universities in the United States. From its classrooms have emerged six American presidents—from John Adams to John F. Kennedy—and an impressive group of statesmen, business leaders, and literary figures. Its campus in Cambridge, Massachusetts, just across the Charles River from Boston, provides a rich architectural mix that includes the ivy-covered brick of Puritan New England and the concrete and glass of contemporary design. The oldest buildings surround Harvard Yard where a statue pays tribute to John Harvard, the English clergyman who was the school's first principal benefactor.

Today, the university includes Harvard and Radcliffe undergraduate colleges, 10 professional schools, the Graduate School of Arts and Sciences, and an extension school. Its enrollment of approximately 1,600 students is drawn from every state and 45 foreign countries; tuition is about $12,000 a year, and 70 percent of those attending receive financial aid.

The university's library system is the largest in the world; it contains more than 10 million volumes and subscribes to 100,000 periodicals. There are three notable art museums—the Fogg Museum of Art, the Busch-Reisinger Museum, and the Arthur M. Sackler Museum—which house works from ancient Egyptian to contemporary American. There are also the Botanical Museum, 40 acres of athletic fields, an experimental forest located in New England, a center for the study of the Italian Renaissance in Italy, and a center for Byzantine studies in Washington, D.C.

Plymouth Rock

In December 1620, after a bitter three-month voyage across the Atlantic Ocean, 128 Pilgrims landed on Cape Cod to establish what would become the oldest continuous settlement in the United States—Plymouth, Massachusetts. Over the succeeding centuries, the granite boulder at which they set anchor has been preserved to commemorate this historic event. Labeled Plymouth Rock, it was approximately 15 feet long and 3 feet wide. In 1774, it was moved to the middle of town (for political reasons), breaking in two in the process. In 1880, it was returned to its original site and the two pieces reunited, although vandalism had reduced its length to about a quarter of its original size. Today, it rests under a portico designed to protect it from further erosion, a gift from the Dames of America in 1920.

Moored nearby is *Mayflower II*, a replica of the tiny wooden ship that was chartered by the Virginia Company of London to carry the Pilgrims to their intended destination, Virginia. Also on the waterfront is First House, an example of the earliest permanent house built by the Pilgrims, and 1627 House, which shows later refinements.

Three miles from Plymouth there is an authentic re-creation of the Pilgrim village, Plimouth Plantation, where costumed interpreters portray members of the 50 families who lived there. There is also a pilgrim museum in Plymouth that claims to be the country's oldest public museum. Among its treasures is John Alden's halberd.

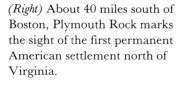

A statue of Massasoit overlooks the portico that houses Plymouth Rock. The enclosure was a gift of the Dames of America in 1920.

(Right) About 40 miles south of Boston, Plymouth Rock marks the sight of the first permanent American settlement north of Virginia.

Niagara Falls

At 3,175 feet wide and 182 feet at their highest point, Niagara Falls, on the border between the United States and Canada, are indeed among the natural wonders of the world. Despite their seemingly immutable presence, the falls actually creep upstream at a rate of one to four feet each year; in 12,000 years, they have moved seven miles.

Almost as famous as Niagara is the "Maid of the Mist" boat ride. In nearly continual operation since the 1840s, it takes tourists through the churning waters at the base of the American and Bridal Veil Falls and nearly under the downpour of Horseshoe Falls. Bridges link the American and Canadian sides, while a glass-enclosed elevator takes visitors to the top of the New York State Observation Tower for a stunning overview. There also are tours available by bus, sightseeing train, and helicopters. The falls are even more spectacular, if possible, at night, when lights play off the mist and water.

Overlooking the falls is Niagara Reservation Park, the first state park in the United States, and home of the Native American Center for the Living Arts. Five miles downstream is the Robert Moses Niagara Power Plant, one of the largest hydroelectric developments in the western hemisphere. From the Power Vista, its public observation building (which is twice as high as the falls), visitors have a panoramic view of Niagara and the surrounding countryside.

(Below) For a close-up view of Niagara, passengers ride the Maid of the Mist where a ticket includes the loan of a raincoat as protection from the falls' spray.

(Right) No photo or painting can truly capture Horseshoe Falls' awesome power and beauty. It is a sight that one must simply see for oneself.

When affairs of state permitted, FDR would retreat to his beloved family home in Hyde Park, NY. America's 32nd president was born there and is buried there.

Hyde Park

This 35-room mansion overlooking the Hudson River Valley was Franklin D. Roosevelt's birthplace, his burial place, and, by all accounts, his favorite place. Its formal name is Springwood, but Roosevelt called it the "Big House." Today it is more commonly called "Hyde Park" for the town in which it is situated.

Built in the early 1800s, the mansion began as a two-story frame building with clapboard siding. FDR and his mother, Sara Delano Roosevelt, had it enlarged in 1915 to accommodate Franklin and Eleanor's five children. FDR was born in the Blue Room, the master bedroom of the smaller house. The bedroom in which he slept as a child was later used by his sons. These and 13 other rooms are open to the public, and, despite a nearly disastrous fire in 1982, all the furnishings, except some of the carpets, wallpaper, and fabrics, are original. The birds he collected are still in a case in the Main Hall; his favorite naval prints and family pictures remain in the bedroom he used as an adult; and the leash and blanket of his dog, Fala, are on the Scottish terrier's chair.

Adjacent to the mansion is the first presidential library, built in 1939, to house the papers, gifts, and memorabilia of America's 32nd president and his wife. Franklin and Eleanor Roosevelt are buried in the rose garden surrounded by a hedge of hemlock. The simple marble tombstone bears only their names and dates of birth and death: Franklin Delano Roosevelt, 1881–1945, and Anna Eleanor Roosevelt, 1884–1962.

West Point

Visitors to the United States Military Academy will find it a blend of campus and museum. Indeed, West Point, with its towering Gothic structures, is the nation's oldest military post in continual operation. Colonial forces drilled here before seeing battle in the Revolutionary War. George Washington supervised construction of the Point's early fortifications, and Thomas Jefferson signed legislation that created the academy in 1802. A roll call of its graduates includes Presidents Ulysses S. Grant and Dwight D. Eisenhower, Generals Robert E. Lee, John J. Pershing, and Douglas MacArthur, and astronauts Edwin E. Aldrin, Jr., E. Frank Borman, and Michael Collins. From its original cadre of 10 cadets, it has grown to an annual enrollment of approximately 4,400 men and women today.

While the barracks, academic buildings, and library are not open to the general public, guests may tour some of the facilities, including the main activities building. Visitors are also welcome at the 1920 Cadet Chapel, which houses the largest church organ in the world, and the Old Cadet Chapel, built in 1836 and moved to its present site in 1911. Visitors also can tour the West Point museum, which contains a collection of military arms from the 16th through 20th centuries, and view war relics dating from the American Revolution at Trophy Point.

The grounds of the academy, which offer a magnificent view of the Hudson River Valley, are dotted with monuments to American military heroes. The American Soldier Statue, created by Felix W. DeWeldon, the sculptor of the Iwo Jima memorial *(see p. 53),* and dedicated in 1980, is a tribute to all American soldiers.

(Top) Looking past the 19th-century cannon, one can glimpse the Point's Gothic buildings and, beyond that, the picturesque Hudson River Valley.

(Above) The long gray line musters on the parade ground today much as it did when Grant, MacArthur, or Eisenhower were cadets.

The Statue of Liberty

Created by the noted French sculptor Frédéric-Auguste Bartholdi and presented as a gift by the people of France to the people of the United States, the Statue of Liberty—or"Liberty Enlightening the World," as she is called officially—stands as a symbol of freedom (and indeed of America) in New York Harbor. Dedicated in 1886, Liberty is 305 feet high from pedestal to torch tip. The statue itself is 151 feet tall and weighs 225 tons; her eyes are 2 feet wide, her nose 4 feet long, and her waist 35 feet around, yet her copper skin is only 3/32-inch thick.

At her base is the American Museum of Immigration, which offers multimedia exhibits on the origins and contribution of immigrants to the United States. An elevator carries passengers to a balcony around the top of the pedestal, and, for the adventuresome, a staircase winding the equivalent of 12 stories leads to Liberty's crown. In honor of her centennial, she underwent a two-year restoration fittingly carried out by a team of French and American workers. When she was rededicated during a four-day gala in July 1986, she proudly displayed a brand-new torch.

The National Park Service estimates that she has been visited by more than 50 million people. Of course, no trip to Miss Liberty would be complete without a reading of the words of poet Emma Lazarus inscribed in the base: "Give me your tired, your poor, / Your huddled masses yearning to breathe free, / The wretched refuse of your teeming shore. / Send these, the homeless, tempest-tossed to me: / I lift my lamp beside the golden door!"

(*Left*) Since 1886, the Statue of Liberty has served as a symbol of American freedom and equality the world over.

(*Below*) The stern countenance of sculptor Auguste Bartholdi's mother served as the model for Liberty's features.

Manhattan

New York is, in many ways, America's premier city. It is the nation's financial, communications, and cultural center. It is the country's largest metropolis, with 7 million people representing a widely diverse mix of ethnic and racial groups. It is the "Big Apple," fabled in song and story, and the site of so many movies and television shows that to many Americans it is as familiar as their own hometown.

While New York is composed of five boroughs, joined in 1898, the place most people come to visit is Manhattan. Here at the lower end is the financial district bordered by Wall Street, the Stock Exchange, and the World Trade Center. A few miles uptown are Soho, teeming with art galleries and boutiques, and Greenwich Village, which offers good restaurants, clubs, and small playhouses.

In midtown, one finds the most familiar sites—Macy's Department Store, Rockefeller Center, Radio City Music Hall, the elegant shops along Fifth Avenue, the fabulous Museum of Modern Art, and Carnegie Hall. Here, too, is the Broadway theatre district and Lincoln Center for the Performing Arts including the Metropolitan Opera. On the East Side stands the United Nations complex.

Further uptown, on the East Side one finds a wealth of art galleries, antique shops, and museums which, in addition to the Metropolitan *(see pp. 28–29),* include the Whitney Museum of American Art and the Solomon R. Guggenheim Museum, designed by Frank Lloyd Wright.

For those who wish to venture out of Manhattan, the other boroughs of New York City offer their share of worthwhile attractions, among them the Brooklyn Museum and the Bronx Zoo.

In 1983, New York celebrated, in typically grand fashion, the 100th birthday of John A. Roebling's engineering triumph, the Brooklyn Bridge.

(Opposite) Once America's premier art deco movie palace, Radio City Music Hall today plays host to concert performers and family-oriented revues, with the Rockettes in frequent attendance.

(Left) Overlooking Rockefeller Center's sunken plaza is Paul Manship's gilded statue, *Prometheus Giving Fire to Mankind.*

(Below) The United Nations complex along the East River houses the General Assembly and the Security Council. The World Court meets in The Hague.

Booth
THE
ELEPHANT
MAN
'RIVETING'
BROADHURST
WHOREHOUSE
PARK
ST. JAMES
Oh! Calcutta!
MAJESTIC
Edison Theatre
SANTORINI
SEA HOUSE
46 St.
ROYALE
PARK
PARAMOUNT
CHORUS LINE
PARK
OPEN 24 HOURS
Dancin
Carlton
Kinney
PARK
BILTMORE
ON RADIO CAL
5F32

(*Above*) The Empire State Building, with its patriotic red, white, and blue light display, is no longer the world's tallest building but no New York visitor wants to miss it. Perhaps they are hoping to glimpse King Kong.

At night, Times Square, in the heart of the Broadway theater district, offers a dazzling combination of lights, action, and bustling excitement.

Giant banners announcing the Metropolitan's special exhibitions add color to the museum's beaux arts facade on Fifth Avenue.

The André Meyer Galleries house the Met's Impressionist masterpieces, a collection unrivaled in size by that of any other museum in the world except the Musée d'Orsay in Paris.

The Metropolitan Museum of Art

The largest art museum in the western hemisphere, the Metropolitan Museum of Art was founded in 1870 by New York City business and civic leaders and moved into its beaux arts building on Fifth Avenue in 1905. Today, it incorporates a maze of exhibition areas whose variety astonishes and occasionally overwhelms, especially when one considers that only a small portion of the vast permanent collection is on display at any one time.

The Egyptian collection alone comprises 18,000 items; its centerpiece is the Temple of Dendur, circa 15 B.C., which once overlooked the Nile River. Arts of antiquity also come from Greece, Rome, and the Near and Far East. Displays of medieval art and armor may be found not only in the main building but also in the museum's upper Manhattan branch, the Cloisters.

The Met's collection of European master paintings—America's most extensive—fills a major portion of the second-floor galleries. This includes a large and very popular group of Impressionist masterpieces. In the American Wing, most of the collection is housed behind the facade of an 1820s New York bank. Here one will find the world's largest collection of American paintings (including Leutz's gigantic icon, *Washington Crossing the Delaware*). There are also 25 period rooms that date from a 1674 colonial parlor to a 1914 living room by Frank Lloyd Wright.

The museum also features comprehensive collections of oriental, primitive, and 20th-century art. In addition, it is renowned for its massive special exhibitions, some of which, like the Degas retrospective in 1988, require special tickets and sell out months in advance.

The Great Hall, directly off of the museum's main entrance, was designed by leading architect Richard Morris Hunt at the turn of the century.

Atlantic City

Atlantic City is the belle of the Jersey Shore, the 127-mile stretch of Atlantic Ocean coastline that sweeps from Sandy Hook to Cape May, New Jersey. While its boardwalk made the city a famed resort in the early part of this century, much of the action has moved indoors since 1978, when the decision to legalize gambling reversed the city's economic decline of the 1950s and 1960s. It became commonplace in the late 1970s to see antique buildings demolished and casinos rise in their place. Today there are 12, including Trump Plaza, Trump's Castle, Tropicana, Caesar's, and the first, Resorts International; nearly all face the boardwalk.

A stroll along that famed wooden walkway today will introduce visitors to an agglomeration of souvenir stands, fast-food carryouts, video arcades, and amusement stalls. It's also a grand place to roller skate, bicycle, jog, and people watch. For those who do not gamble, the casinos also offer excellent opportunities to people watch—famous people, that is—for all of the major casino-hotels have large showrooms where such performers as Frank Sinatra, Bill Cosby, Eddie Murphy, Don Rickles, and Liza Minnelli regularly appear.

Atlantic City is also an excellent spot for saltwater fishing; more than 30 species exist here. With its gently sloping beach, it's also ideal for swimming, and the literally thousands of shipwrecks offshore make it a divers' mecca.

Since the first gambling casino opened in 1978, Atlantic City has changed from a sleepy resort town to an east coast hot spot with more than 31 million guests a year.

Independence National Historical Park

To walk through Independence National Historical Park is to retrace the steps of those who brought the United States to life. For here, on the edge of downtown Philadelphia, is a collection of buildings in which the Founding Fathers created the Declaration of Independence, mounted an army to fight the British, and drafted the Constitution.

In Carpenters Hall, the First Continental Congress met in 1774, and delegates spoke openly—and treasonously—of using force to gain independence from Great Britain. In Independence Hall, the Second Continental Congress, meeting in 1775, named George Washington commander-in-chief of the Continental Army, and, in 1776, signed the Declaration of Independence. In this same hall in 1787, the Constitution of the new United States was adopted. Next door, in Congress Hall, the newly formed legislative body met from 1790 to 1800; Presidents Washington and John Adams were inaugurated here as well. Today, furnishings from the period are on view in Carpenters Hall, while Independence Hall displays the silver inkstand delegates used to sign the Declaration of Independence and the chair in which Washington sat during the Constitutional Convention.

The most revered symbol of that tumultuous time, the Liberty Bell, can be seen in a glass-enclosed pavilion near Independence Hall. The bell, which had hung in the hall's belfry since 1753, and which had summoned Philadelphians to hear the first reading of the Declaration of Independence, was moved to its present site for America's Bicentennial in 1976. The bell atop the tower of the park's visitor center was cast by the same English foundry and was a Bicentennial gift from Queen Elizabeth II.

(Opposite) The cornerstones of American democracy, the Declaration of Independence and the Constitution were drafted in Independence Hall, perhaps the most historic building in the United States.

The Assembly Room in Independence Hall has been re-created to look as it did in 1776 when the Declaration of Independence was signed.

(Following page) No longer hanging from the belfry of Independence Hall, the Liberty Bell is now on view in its own glass-enclosed pavilion on grounds that once housed the president's mansion.

Fallingwater

Fallingwater, perhaps the best-known residential work in Frank Lloyd Wright's long and distinguished career, is nestled in the wooded hills of southeastern Pennsylvania about two hours from Pittsburgh. Designed in 1936, when the architect was 67 years old, the three-story residence was, for 26 years, the weekend home of Pittsburgh department store owner Edgar J. Kaufmann and his family.

At the heart of the design is a cantilevered beam system that allows the house to extend beyond its supports and to literally thrust out and over the waterfall for which it is named. Wright's plan includes a series of broad terraces that echo the site's rocky ledges, and intersecting planes of fractured sandstone that are reminiscent of the surrounding bluffs. "I think you can hear the waterfall when you look at the design," Wright said.

The plan also includes a few whimsical touches, such as a glass hatch in the living room. It leads to a set of exterior hanging stairs and from there to the water below.

In 1963, the Kaufmann's son, Edgar Jr., donated the house to the Western Pennsylvania Conservancy. He said of it, "Such a place cannot be possessed. It is a work by man for man, not by a man for a man." Vincent Scully of Yale University calls it "one of the most complete masterpieces of twentieth-century art." It is the only Wright house with its setting, original furnishings, and art work intact. In addition to the main building, there is a guest house and office on the hill above, also designed by Wright.

(*Top*) Fallingwater extends out and over Bear Run Falls, giving perfect expression to Frank Lloyd Wright's belief that a building should complement its natural surroundings.

(*Above*) The living room/study features original furnishings designed by the architect.

Gettysburg National Military Park

On three days in July 1863, the Confederate forces of General Robert E. Lee met the Union soldiers of General George G. Meade near the small Pennsylvania town of Gettysburg. More than 51,000 casualties fell in this, the climactic battle of the Civil War, a battle in which more men were killed and wounded than in any other military engagement in North America. For the South, the battle was decisive. Lee's army, exhausted physically and spiritually, would never again penetrate the North, and Gettysburg would come to be known as the "high-water mark of the Confederacy."

Four months after the battle, President Abraham Lincoln came to Gettysburg to dedicate a cemetery for the Union dead. His two-minute speech, the Gettysburg Address, is one of the masterpieces of English writing.

Visitors to the park can follow the course of the battle either by car or on foot as markers describe significant engagements. At the visitor's center, colored lights illustrate troop movements on an electric map while, on the battlefield, remnants recall the carnage: a barricade of boulders that shielded a Confederate sharpshooter at Devil's Den; part of an artillery battery along the High Water Mark Trail. At the Cyclorama Center nearby, a circular painting accompanied by a sound-and-light program describes the ill-fated charge of 12,000 Confederates led by General George E. Pickett.

During the summer, the center displays one of the two draft copies of Lincoln's Gettysburg Address. Contrary to legend, he did not write his speech on the back of an envelope en route to the dedication; he prepared it, taking great pains with its composition, before leaving Washington.

The high ground of Cemetery Hill served as a place of refuge for the Union cavalry at the end of the first day of battle, July 1, 1863.

The cannons are silent now but, during the crucial battle of Gettysburg, approximately 50,000 Union and Confederate soldiers lost their lives.

Fort McHenry

Named for James McHenry, secretary of war under Presidents George Washington and John Adams, Fort McHenry saw battle only once, during the War of 1812, but that occasion gave rise to America's national anthem.

Completed in the late 1790s, Fort McHenry met history in September 1814 when it was attacked by the British navy during the War of 1812. For 25 hours, the garrison was subjected to intensive shellfire. Despite the battering, however, the fort held, with only four Americans killed and 24 wounded. An attorney, Francis Scott Key, who had been confined by the British to a vessel in Chesapeake Bay, saw at dawn that the American flag still flew above the fort and was inspired to write, "O say can you see, by the dawn's early light . . . " This poem, later set to the music of a drinking song, became America's national anthem, "The Star Spangled Banner."

The main portion of the garrison, Star Fort, takes its name from its starlike shape, based on a century-old French design. During the Civil War, it was used as a prison for Confederate soldiers and it became an army hospital during World War I. In 1925, it was dedicated a national park.

What remains of the 1814 fort are the dry moat that protected some of its defenders, and a V-shaped outerwork that sheltered the entrance from direct attack; from the bastion, one can still view the Patapsco River, where the British fleet lay at anchor. The officers' quarters, the barracks, and the powder magazine have been restored, and, on the site of the original flagpole, a new one stands. From it, a star-spangled banner yet waves.

Inner Harbor offers visitors a host of activities, from elegant dining to boutique shopping to a tour of the frigate U.S.S. *Constellation,* launched in 1797.

Inner Harbor

In the 1970s, the city of Baltimore began a massive redevelopment program to reclaim its historic harbor front from the deserted warehouses and decaying docks that had come to dominate the area. Today, shoppers, visitors to the city, and business people mix in a lively glass-and-steel environment whose heart is Harborplace. Its two pavilions, skywalks, and 28-story mixed-use Gallery include the Colonnade Market, which offers produce, cheese, fish, and meat; the Food Hall, which features small eateries serving international dishes; and the two-story Trading Center, which sells baked goods, gourmet foods, and wines. Eating at Harborplace offers a dazzling array of choices. There are Szechuan, Mandarin, Greek, Indian, French, and Italian restaurants, as well as those with regional

menus; seafood is a specialty, especially crab.

About 135 businesses operate in Harborplace and another 75 in the Gallery. They range from nationally known retailers to local crafts people selling unique merchandise.

Within a few minutes' walk from Harborplace are a host of diverse attractions. Among them are the highly regarded National Aquarium and the Maryland Science Center. Two sailing ships, the U.S.S. *Constellation* and the *Pride of Baltimore*, are berthed in the harbor. And the nearby World Trade Center has an observation deck that provides a panoramic view of the city and the Chesapeake Bay.

(Following pages) Horse-drawn carriages, complete with liveried drivers, enhance the 18th-century atmosphere of Colonial Williamsburg.

The
Southeast

Washington, D.C.

Carved out of small portions of Maryland and Virginia to form the nation's capital in 1800 (succeeding New York and Philadelphia), Washington, D.C., is a magnet that draws people from all over the world. Here are the centers of the government's three branches: the Capitol, begun in 1793; the White House, home to every president except George Washington; and the Supreme Court, completed in 1935. All are open for tours, as are a number of other public buildings including the Federal Bureau of Investigation

(Opposite) The magnificent tiered dome of the U.S. Capitol was erected during the Civil War, replacing a less imposing structure by Charles Bulfinch.

and the Bureau of Engraving and Printing.

Washington is a city of monuments, and its most famous pay tribute to Presidents Washington, Jefferson, and Lincoln. There is also the Vietnam Veterans Memorial, which has become the city's most-visited monument since its dedication in 1982. Washington is a city of museums as well. These include the vast Smithsonian Institution *(see pp. 48–51)*; the National Gallery of Art, which houses one of the nation's finest collections of paintings, sculptures, drawings, and prints; the National Archives, where the original copies of the Declaration of Independence and the Constitution are displayed; the Corcoran Museum, which features an im-

pressive collection of American painting and sculpture; and the Phillips Collection, the first museum of modern art in the country.

Among Washington's other treasures are Ford's Theatre, where Lincoln was shot; and the Folger Library, with the world's largest collection of Shakespeareana. The city also offers a wide array of excellent shops and restaurants, many in Georgetown, the city's oldest section, founded in 1751.

From the great lawn, one can see the oval south portico of the White House, added by the mansion's original architect, James Hoban, in 1824.

In the rotunda of the Jefferson Memorial stands a 19-foot statue of the third U.S. president by Rudolph Evans.

Surrounded by excerpts from his second inaugural address, Daniel Chester French's Lincoln gazes benignly upon those who pay homage at his memorial.

Designed by Maya Ying Lin, the Vietnam
Veterans Memorial contains the names of
the 58,312 Americans killed in the conflict.

(*Opposite*) The 555-foot monument to
George Washington, seen here from the
Lincoln Memorial, was begun in 1848 and
completed 40 years later.

Many of those who lost friends or relatives
in Vietnam trace the names of their loved
ones with paper and pencil supplied on the
site.

The Smithsonian Institution

In 1835, British scientist James Smithson left his entire fortune, then worth about a half-million dollars, to the United States for the purpose of creating an institution "for the increase and diffusion of knowledge among men." Why he did so remains a mystery. His legacy, the Smithsonian Institution, today comprises 14 museums and galleries, the National Zoo in Washington, D.C., and an array of research facilities. Affectionately referred to as the "nation's attic," the Smithsonian presently houses an estimated 135 million objects, works of art, specimens, and animals.

Nine of the Smithsonian museums are on the Mall between the United States Capitol and the Washington Monument. The most popular is the National Air and Space Museum, which annually draws more visitors than any other museum in the world, and whose exhibits include the original Wright Flyer, Lindbergh's "Spirit of St. Louis," the Apollo II command module, and a moon rock that visitors can touch.

Also on the Mall are the National Museum of American History, whose treasures include the Star-Spangled Banner, the gowns of the first ladies, and Archie Bunker's chair; and the National Museum of Natural History, whose dinosaur remains and giant stuffed elephant (in the rotunda) serve to delight visitors of all ages.

For art lovers, the Smithsonian offers a wide range of choices, including the Freer Gallery (Asian art), the Hirshhorn Museum and Sculpture Garden (contemporary painting and sculpture), and the National Museum of American Art. The Cooper-Hewitt Museum, the National Museum of Design, is in New York.

The Smithsonian Castle, erected in the 1840s and 1850s, once housed all of the Institution's collections. Now it primarily serves as an administrative facility.

(*Opposite top*) In the entrance hall of the National Air and Space Museum, visitors can see nearly a century of milestones, from the Wright Brothers' original flyer (*upper foreground*) to John Glenn's Mercury space capsule, *Friendship 7 (lower foreground).*

(*Opposite bottom*) The National Museum of American History displays first ladies' gowns set against the White House's changing decor. Shown here are the dresses of Mrs. Harding through Mrs. Eisenhower in a replica of the early-20th-century East Room.

The Smithsonian Institution includes 14 museums, nine of which are located on the National Mall between the Washington Monument and the Capitol.

Arlington National Cemetery

Arlington National Cemetery has been called the nation's most hallowed burial ground. Here on a hillside in Virginia across the Potomac River from Washington, D.C., lie 200,000 Americans, known and unknown, representing every war in America's history, from the Revolution to Vietnam.

Among the honored dead are President John F. Kennedy, his grave lit by an eternal flame and ringed with quotations from his 1961 inaugural address. Nearby is the burial place of his brother, Robert, who was assassinated in 1968, five years after the President. Among other notables buried here are President William Howard Taft; Chief Justice of the Supreme Court Earl Warren; heavyweight boxing champion Joe Louis; and General John J. "Black Jack" Pershing.

A focal point of the annual Memorial Day observances is the Tomb of the Unknown Soldier, a victim of World War I buried on the Memorial Amphitheatre plaza in 1921. Since then, unidentified soldiers symbolizing World War II, the Korean Conflict, and the Vietnam Conflict have been interred here. The site is guarded perpetually by a sentinel from the "Old Guard," the U.S. Third Infantry.

Overlooking the cemetery is Arlington House, the neoclassical home of Confederate General Robert E. Lee built in the early 1800s. Seized at the outset of the war, the property became a burial ground for Union soldiers. Visitors can tour the mansion, which became a national monument to Lee in 1955.

An eternal flame marks the burial place of John Fitzgerald Kennedy, 35th president of the United States. Overlooking the grave site is the Custis-Lee mansion.

(*Right*) The Tomb of the Unknown Soldier honors U.S. Army casualties of World Wars I and II, the Korean Conflict and the Vietnam Conflict.

(*Opposite*) Based on a photograph by Joseph Rosenthal, the Statue of Iwo Jima, just outside the cemetery, depicts five marines raising the American flag on Mount Suribachi during World War II.

HERE RESTS IN
HONORED GLORY
AN AMERICAN
SOLDIER
KNOWN BUT TO GOD

Mount Vernon

(Opposite) From the air one can see the small buildings, called dependencies, that are adjacent to the mansion. They include a stable, carriage house, and slave quarters.

A semicircular colonnade connects the main house to the kitchen, which was maintained separately to protect the living quarters from heat and cooking odors.

George Washington's beloved Mount Vernon, the Virginia plantation 16 miles east of the city that bears his name, has been painstakingly restored to appear as it did in 1799, when the first president died. Begun about 1735 by his father, the mansion is the centerpiece of 30 acres of gardens and wooded grounds open to visitors. Built of wood and painted to resemble stone block, the two-story home with its portico of columns overlooks the Potomac River valley; on the mansion's opposite side is an expansive bowling green developed by Washington in 1785 and on which some of the original trees survive.

Washington acquired the estate in 1754 when he was 22. From then until his death, he oversaw Mount Vernon's growth to 8,000 acres divided into five farms, each with its own slaves, livestock, buildings, and equipment. The 500 acres owned today by the Mount Vernon Ladies' Association approximate the boundaries of the Mansion House Farm. Washington himself determined the location of the outbuildings, and visitors can see the kitchen, smokehouse, spinning house, coach house, and stable, all furnished with implements from the period.

Three gardens still flourish: the upper garden, with boxwood planted in Washington's day; the kitchen garden; and the botanical garden where Washington experimented with seeds and plants not native to Virginia. A greenhouse and orangerie, flanked by slave quarters, was destroyed by fire in the 1800s but has been reconstructed. In the mansion, 14 rooms are shown; many of the furnishings are original and arranged as they were when the Washingtons lived there. Throughout, the colors of the walls reflect the president's choices.

Washington and his wife Martha are buried at Mount Vernon, and their mausoleum is also on view.

The portico overlooks the Potomac River offering a view that is as splendid today as it was when Washington knew it.

The dining room features a revolving service door with shelves so servants did not have to leave the kitchen during meals *(not pictured)*. The archway *(right)* leads to a small tea room.

An alcove bed, open on both sides, separates Jefferson's dressing room from his study.

Monticello

Monticello, designed by Thomas Jefferson, is considered one of America's outstanding examples of neoclassical architecture.

Monticello in Italian means "little mountain," and, indeed, that is where the home of Thomas Jefferson, third president of the United States, is situated—atop an 867-foot peak near Charlottesville, Virginia. One of the premier examples of American neoclassicism, it was designed by its owner, a man of many talents, who once wrote, "Architecture is my delight, and putting up and pulling down one of my favorite amusements." It has been said that no house so reflects the interests of its occupant as this one, which he built and rebuilt over 40 years.

Centered on 5,000 acres of land that Jefferson inherited when he was 14 years old, Monticello is modeled after the designs of the 16th-century Italian architect Andrea Palladio. Jefferson began work on the house in 1769 when he was 26, but it was unfinished when he went to France in 1784. Nine years later, when he retired temporarily from public service, he returned to Monticello, which he greatly enlarged. Today, guests can visit all of the major rooms on the main floor, including the entrance hall where Jefferson displayed fossils, native-American artifacts, and a seven-day clock. The grounds, which are being restored from his detailed records, are also open to view.

A woodland trail leads to his grave site. Of his many accomplishments, he ordered that only three be noted on his marker: that he wrote the Declaration of Independence; that he wrote the statute of religious freedom for Virginia; and that he founded the University of Virginia. As he wished, there is no mention of his presidency.

Colonial Williamsburg

Sixty years ago, Williamsburg was just another quiet 20th-century village. Today, thanks to an exhaustive restoration program begun in 1926 by John D. Rockefeller and the town rector, Rev. W. A. R. Goodwin, Williamsburg faithfully re-creates colonial America on the brink of revolution. As Virginia's capital, Williamsburg was at the heart of the conflict, and the names associated with it are a roll call of patriots: George Washington, Thomas Jefferson, Patrick Henry, George Mason, Peyton Randolph.

The 173-acre Historic Area contains nearly ninety 18th-century restorations, including homes, shops, taverns, and other public places. Scores of other buildings, large and small, have been re-created on their original sites, as have approximately 90 acres of gardens and public greens. A walk down the Duke of Gloucester Street, the main thoroughfare that connects the Capitol to the College of William and Mary, is a walk back in time. The street bustles with liveried coaches, with craftsmen and women busily engaged in chores, and with children rolling 18th-century hoops. Visitors are invited to enter shops and some of the homes, where costumed interpreters discuss everyday life 200 years ago. In many of the shops, craftspeople demonstrate trades such as blacksmithing, printing, and wigmaking. In addition, merchants offer goods similar to those sold in colonial times (including those that the village craftspeople produce), while the taverns provide authentic menus in their restored dining rooms.

Visitors also may tour two museums, the DeWitt Wallace Decorative Arts Gallery, which houses an impressive array of furniture, ceramics, and metal work, and the Abby Aldrich Rockefeller Folk Art Center, which exhibits an outstanding collection of American primitive art.

The Governor's Palace housed seven royal representatives and the commonwealth's first two chief executives. This is a 1930s recreation of the original, which burned in 1781.

Through more than 30 crafts demonstrations, artisans, like this cooper, explain to visitors the fundamental structure of the 18th-century economy — how goods were created, sold, and used.

The Capitol, which housed a bicameral legislature, saw many a fiery debate in the 1770s, including Patrick Henry's rabble-rousing orations against the Stamp Act.

Costumed interpreters, like this town crier, help 20th-century visitors understand the customs and behavior of colonial America.

It took years to remove two centuries of modernization and return Duke of Gloucester Street to its 18th-century appearance.

Busch Gardens, The Old Country

At the gate of Busch Gardens, The Old Country, visitors leave behind the lush Williamsburg, Virginia, countryside and enter a 360-acre family entertainment park that takes its cue from four of Europe's principal nations.

Directly past the entrance is the English hamlet of Banbury Cross, whose main attractions are a petting zoo and an ice-skating show, housed in a theater modeled on Shakespeare's Globe. Next door is Heatherdowns, a Scottish village that is home to the "Loch Ness Monster," a 13-story roller coaster with a pair of interlocking loops. Across a drawbridge is Hastings, another English village that offers a musical revue, a computer-animated show, and Renaissance games of skill.

In "France," the quaint village of Aquitaine boasts a 5,200-seat theater that plays host to such entertainers as Johnny Mathis, Jay Leno, and the Oak Ridge Boys. There are also Le Mans, where aspiring Mario Andrettis can maneuver mini-racers, and New France, a Canadian fur-trappers' village where a flume ride sends occupants plunging down a 50-foot fall. Rhinefeld, in the heart of "Germany," offers Rhine River cruises, an antique carousel, and gemütlichkeit at a typical German beer hall. Finally, there's "Italy" and the village of San Marco where DaVinci's inventive drawings find life as action-packed rides, where Festa Italia re-creates a street carnival based on Marco Polo's travels, and where the park's newest ride, Roman Rapids, hurtles guests through the ruins of the ancient capital.

For the less adventuresome, each village offers shops and restaurants that also evoke the charm of Old World Europe.

A happy burgermeister welcomes visitors to Rhinefeld, one of the charming villages in Busch Gardens, The Old Country.

Visitors can board a paddle-driven sidewheeler for a cruise down the "Rhine" *(foreground)*, or ride the "Loch Ness Monster" *(rear)* for a less relaxing journey.

Modeled after the beer halls of Munich, the massive Festhaus features folk dancers, an oompah band, and authentic German food.

Churchill Downs

Each year, on the first Saturday in May, an average of 20 million television viewers tune in to watch what has been called "the greatest two minutes in sports"—the running of the Kentucky Derby. This spring classic is held at perhaps the most celebrated race track in America, Churchill Downs.

Originally called the Louisville Jockey Club and Driving Club Association, Churchill Downs was founded in 1874 by Colonel M. Lewis Clark. On May 17, 1875, a little red horse named Aristides won the first Derby. While the grandstands, grounds, and clubhouse have changed over the years, the track remains essentially the same. But the attention paid to and the stakes associated with the Derby have changed dramatically. Instead of the 10,000 fans who saw the first "Run for the Roses," 100,000 now fill the famed Twin Spires grandstand (built in 1894) and the oval infield. And, instead of Aristides' purse of $2,850, the winner of the 1988 Derby, Winning Colors, took home more than $611,000.

The complex recently underwent a $23 million renovation. It now includes the Kentucky Derby Museum, which opened in 1985 and features a 360-degree film presentation, computer-simulated racing and trivia games, and information on Derby winners. There are also displays of hundreds of racing items, and a thoroughbred is stabled on the museum's grounds.

Churchill Downs also is noted for its floral displays, and, except for tulips imported from Holland, the nearly 60,000 flowers planted each year are grown in the race course's own greenhouses. In 1987, the clubhouse garden became the site of a special bronze statue—a larger-than-life sculpture of Aristides.

On Derby Day the eyes of the nation turn toward Churchill Downs where approximately 100,000 spectators fill Twin Spires grandstand and the oval infield.

Graceland

One-half hour from downtown Memphis, the complex that commemorates one of America's most popular singers draws hundreds of thousands of visitors annually. Graceland, the southern colonial-style fieldstone mansion that was Elvis Presley's home for 20 years, was opened as a museum in 1982. Visitors can view several of the home's 23 rooms, including Presley's favorite, his den, which he decorated with furnishings bought on a half-hour shopping spree in a Memphis store. Also on display is a collection of his vehicles, the most famous of which are the 1955 pink Cadillac that he bought for his mother, and the Jeep from his film *Blue Hawaii.* In the trophy room, an 80-foot-long "Hall of Gold" includes his gold and platinum records and the awards attesting to his popularity—more than one billion copies of his records have been sold; no other individual or group in the history of the recording industry has sold more.

Across Elvis Presley Boulevard, the entertainer's two airplanes and his recreational bus are open for tours. The "Lisa Marie," named for his daughter, is a 96-seat passenger jet customized into "an airborne penthouse" in 1975 at a cost of nearly $900,000. The "Hound Dog II" is a smaller private jet. In Graceland Plaza, there is a theater showing film footage from Presley's career as well as additional exhibit areas, gift shops, and eateries, including one called the "Heartbreak Hotel Restaurant."

Near the mansion is the Meditation Garden where Presley, his parents, and his grandmother are buried. The entertainer's headstone is inscribed with a tribute by his father, who wrote, after the singer's death at age 42 in 1977, "We miss you, son. . . ."

(Top) Built in 1939, the 23-room mansion was purchased by Elvis Presley in 1957 for approximately $100,000.

(Above) Elvis, who died in 1977, is buried in the Meditation Garden, a short walk from Graceland.

Opryland USA

The Grand Ole Opry, the longest-running radio show in the United States, took to the airwaves in 1943. Since the 1970s, the venerable music institution has been housed at Opryland USA, a 120-acre musical-entertainment theme park near Nashville. Visitors with tickets can be part of the Opry studio audience and watch top country-music stars as they perform every Friday and Saturday night. Visitors can also participate in a television variety talk show and a radio talk show, watch the taping of television's "Hee Haw," and make their own recordings in a ministudio. Opryland also offers more than a dozen musical revues, featuring young performers recruited through national auditions, and a selection of thrill rides, including one known as the "Screamin' Delta Demon."

In downtown Nashville, the original home of the Grand Ole Opry, Ryman Auditorium continues to play a significant role in country-western lore. Visitors can stand on the stage of the national historic landmark, visit the dressing rooms, and examine the sets, props, and microphones used by legendary country singers. Along nearby Music Row, once the location of block after block of recording studios, the Country Music Hall of Fame and Museum proudly displays related memorabilia, including Minnie Pearl's first hat, the lyrics of Willie Nelson's "Mama, Don't Let Your Babies Grow Up to Be Cowboys," written on the back of a grocery list, and Elvis Presley's gold Cadillac (complete with gold-plated color television). There are also two theaters showing rare film and television footage.

(*Opposite*) One of more than a dozen shows in Opryland, *Music! Music! Music!* stars Brenda Lee in a salute to the sounds of Nashville, Broadway, and Hollywood.

(*Top*) The Ryman Auditorium, now listed in the National Register of Historic Places, was home to the Grand Ole Opry from 1943 to 1974.

(*Above*) The stage of the Grand Ole Opry, where Country Music's best perform every weekend.

The Biltmore Estate

In the Blue Ridge Mountains near Asheville, North Carolina, Biltmore House, a European-style mansion with 250 rooms, rises above the French Broad River as it flows through acres of meticulously landscaped grounds. Biltmore was the country estate of George W. Vanderbilt, grandson of the industrialist Cornelius Vanderbilt. The largest private residence in the United States, it was begun by architect Richard Morris Hunt in 1890 and took hundreds of workers five years to complete.

Visitors are allowed to roam the mansion at their own pace, to view such rooms as the 72-foot-long banquet hall; the 90-foot-long gallery, hung with Brussels tapestries; the 20,000-volume library; the billiard room, with a gaming table used by Napoleon in exile on St. Helena; several of the mansion's 31 bedrooms; the bowling alley; and the trophy room. Throughout, masterpieces of the fine and decorative arts abound, including furniture by Sheraton and Chippendale; paintings by Renoir, Whistler, and Sargent; fine porcelains; and Oriental rugs.

Below stairs, visitors can see the practical side of the household, including three kitchens and the servants' quarters. The grounds—also open to view—offer a stunning array of manicured and informal gardens designed by the creator of New York's Central Park, Frederick Law Olmstead. Visitors may also wish to visit the Biltmore Estate Winery, opened in 1985 in buildings that were originally part of the dairy.

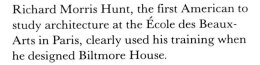

Richard Morris Hunt, the first American to study architecture at the École des Beaux-Arts in Paris, clearly used his training when he designed Biltmore House.

The sunken Palm Court features flowers and greenery grown on the estate, with a fountain and statue by Viennese sculptor Karl Bitter.

The centerpiece of Stone Mountain Park is Borglum's 90- by 190-foot relief sculpture of Jefferson Davis, "Stonewall" Jackson, and Robert E. Lee.

Stone Mountain Park

A granite monolith 825 feet high, Stone Mountain rests like a blue-gray beached whale on a wooded plateau east of Atlanta, Georgia. Surrounded by a 3,200-acre park, the mountain, estimated to be 300 million years old, is the backdrop for the world's largest relief sculpture featuring the likenesses of Confederate President Jefferson Davis and Generals Robert E. Lee and Thomas "Stonewall" Jackson on horseback. Begun in 1923 by American sculptor John Gutzon de la Mothe Borglum, who later designed Mount Rushmore *(see pp. 116–117)*, the 90- by-190-foot work was not completed until 1970. Two cable cars ferry passengers to the top of the mountain, and, at the base, a taped commentary in Memorial Hall tells the history of the carving and explains the geology of the rock.

Throughout the park, visitors are reminded of the South's rich heritage.

There is a replica of a Civil War steam train, which makes a 5-mile circuit around the monolith, and a paddle-wheeler, *The Scarlett O'Hara*, which cruises a 363-acre lake. There is also an authentic reproduction of a cotton plantation, its buildings gathered on the site from a variety of Georgia locales. And there is "The War in Georgia," a sound-and-light show, which re-creates the march to the sea of Civil War Union General William Tecumseh Sherman.

Other attractions include an Antique Auto and Music Museum, a 20-acre refuge for native animals, an 18-hole golf course, two stocked lakes, miles of trails, tennis courts, and water-fun rides. In addition, there are such seasonal events as the annual Stone Mountain Scottish Festival and Highland Games in October.

Walt Disney World

In 1966, Walt Disney unveiled his plan to build a complete family vacation center, including a prototypical community of the future, in a vast new complex near Orlando, Florida. Sadly, he died one week after the announcement, but those who followed carried out his dream and, in 1971, Walt Disney World opened. Since then more than 750 million kids-of-all-ages have visited this charming place.

The complex, occupying 43 acres, includes two resort hotels (the Contemporary and Polynesian Village), campgrounds, a golf course, and the "Magic Kingdom," patterned after Disneyland *(see pp. 144–147)*. Its most recent attraction, "Mickey's Birthday Land," opened in 1989 in honor of the famed mouse's 60th anniversary.

In 1982, a second theme park opened, called EPCOT Center (for Experimental Prototypical Community of Tomorrow). Drawing its inspiration from Walt's vision of a harmonious state-of-the-art community, the park is divided into two sections. The first, "Future World," offers attractions that trace technological developments, delve into the creative process, and explore the land and the sea. The second section, "World Showcase," highlights the life and culture of 10 different nations, from Canada to Japan.

In keeping with Walt's hope that Disney World would constantly grow and change, a third theme park opened in 1989. Called "Disney-MGM," it takes visitors behind the scenes to see how television and movies are created in a working production studio.

Main Street USA, with a horsedrawn trolley in the foreground, points the way toward Cinderella's Castle and, beyond that, Fantasyland.

The Big Bad Wolf and the Three Little Pigs join other Disney characters in a colorful parade through the Magic Kingdom.

(Left) A highlight of any child's visit to the Magic Kingdom is a meeting with Dumbo, or one of the other Disney favorites.

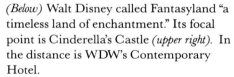

(Below) Walt Disney called Fantasyland "a timeless land of enchantment." Its focal point is Cinderella's Castle *(upper right)*. In the distance is WDW's Contemporary Hotel.

The symbol of EPCOT Center is Spaceship Earth, the world's largest geosphere. Inside, visitors embark on an Audio-Animatronic journey through the history of communication, presented by AT&T.

In EPCOT's World Showcase, visitors reach "China" through a giant ceremonial gate. Beyond is the Hall of Prayer for Good Harvests, which features a 360-degree film on the world's most populous nation.

Busch Gardens, The Dark Continent

Busch Gardens, The Dark Continent, near Tampa, Florida, plunges visitors into the heart of Africa, uniquely combining one of the nation's largest zoos with entertainment, rides, shops, and restaurants in a theme-park setting.

In "Timbuktu", modeled after an ancient desert trading center, guests can enjoy performing dolphins and a sea lion at Dolphin Theater. There are also thrill rides, a carousel, a German fest house, and an African crafts bazaar. The walled city of "Morocco" features a snake charmer, belly dancers, and a marching band as well as a lavish Broadway-style revue. On the "Serengeti Plain," visitors can board a variety of transport vehicles, including a monorail and steam locomotive, to watch a herd of African big game

in a 60-acre veldt. Nearby, elephants, flamingoes, ostriches, dromedaries, and crocodiles are on view. In "Nairobi," there is an animal nursery and petting zoo, while in "Stanleyville," a variety of trained animals perform in a charming show. In this lively village, guests can also take a leisurely cruise on the *African Queen* or a more action-packed trip down a log flume. Finally, Claw Island in the "Congo" features rare white bengal tigers and the notorious "Python," a 1,200-foot roller coaster with a double spiral, while Bird Canyon houses 2,000 feathered creatures representing 224 species.

Adjacent to Busch Gardens is Adventure Island, a separate 13-acre water entertainment park.

(Opposite) The Scorpion in "Timbuktu" takes adventurous guests on a nail-biting journey that includes a 360-degree loop.

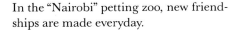

In the "Nairobi" petting zoo, new friendships are made everyday.

The Everglades

At Florida's southernmost tip, the Everglades National Park invites visitors to explore a complex web of environments. Its 1.4 million acres encompass pinelands and hardwood hammocks; cypress and mangrove swamps; marl and coastal prairies; and marine areas and estuaries. Throughout, animal life—both tropical and temperate—abounds. These include birds, such as the great white heron; reptiles, such as the alligator, crocodile, and green sea turtle; and mammals, such as the Florida panther and roundtail muskrat.

Among the best ways to sample the Everglades' rich natural heritage is to take one of the park's numerous walking trails. They range from easy (a quarter-mile) to strenuous (14 miles). One of the most popular is the Anhinga Trail, named for a resident bird. It provides a good opportunity to see a variety of wildlife at close range. Another well-traveled route, the Pa-hay-okee Overlook Trail, features an observation tower with a fine view of the vast river of grass from which the park takes its name. To explore marine areas, visitors can canoe along a variety of trails; the longest, the Wilderness Waterway, twists along the coast for 99 miles from the Flamingo Visitor's Center on Florida Bay to the park's northwestern edge.

Other sightseeing opportunities include talks, demonstrations, canoe trips, and tram tours provided by park naturalists. There are special daily activities as well. These can include slough slogs, dawn bird-watching treks, and other adventures. Overnight camping is allowed provided one has a permit. They are issued on a first-come, first-served basis.

The chance to see rare birds in a lush tropical setting is a lure for many of the park's one million annual visitors.

(Left) The "river of grass"— named for its covering layer of Mangrove leaves — is only 6 inches deep but its shallow waters play host to human- and motor-powered craft.

Kennedy Space Center's Spaceport USA

Kennedy Space Center, on the edge of the Atlantic Ocean east of Orlando, Florida, is the home of the U.S. space program. Here, Kennedy Space Center's Spaceport USA provides glimpses into NASA's history and operations. Its extensive complex features exhibits on the evolution of the program, movies that highlight the space adventure, and more than 250 related paintings, photographs, and sculptures. Throughout the center, actual craft—such as Gemini 9 and the Apollo that docked with a Soviet Soyuz—are on display, as are models of others.

The most spectacular film, *The Dream Is Alive*, which includes footage shot by astronauts in space, is shown on a special screen five-and-a-half stories high and 70-feet wide. The most spectacular exhibit, "Satellites and You," employs audio-animatronic figures and audio-visual effects to simulate working conditions on the space station.

Two guided bus tours are offered. One goes to Cape Canaveral Air Force Station, where the initial manned flights were launched, and provides an overview of the space program's early history. The other tours Kennedy Space Center, site of the present missions. It includes a sight-and-sound show with a real Lunar Module in a simulation of the moon's surface. There is also a stop at Complex 39, launch site for Skylab, the space shuttle, and the Apollo voyages to the moon. A new nature exhibit also uses audio-animatronics to introduce visitors to the wildlife that shares the space center reservation with those who seek adventure beyond this planet.

(Right) Guarding the arrival to Spaceport USA is a "rocket garden" of towering projectiles representing various stages in the US space program.

(Below) These visitors to Spaceport USA get a special treat as they drive past a launch site for the space shuttle.

The Central Region

(Previous pages) Remarkably, Eero Saarinen's majestic Gateway Arch in St. Louis rises to a height of 630 feet solely on the strength of its two triangular legs.

The gleeming white Wrigley Building, home of the Wrigley Chewing Gum Company, has been a celebrated Chicago landmark since its dedication in 1921.

Chicago

Chicago, the nation's third largest city, is home to an estimated three million people, the world's tallest building, and the nation's busiest airport. It is also the Midwest's premier financial and transportation center, a treasure trove of architectural riches, and the site of several excellent museums. Depending upon whom you talk to, its nickname the "Windy City" either reflects the speech of its politicians or the gusts that blow in off Lake Michigan. The lakefront, Chicago's front yard, boasts eight parks (of the city's 600) and several beaches along its 26 miles. Among the jutting

skyscrapers that distinguish Chicago's skyline is the world's tallest building, the 110-story Sears Tower. Other "cloud-piercers" include the John Hancock Building, which, like Sears, has a public observaton deck.

Many landmarks are on or near Lake Michigan, including the 1921 Wrigley Building, whose white terra-cotta facade embellished with baroque ornamentation gleams at night; the Art Institute of Chicago *(see pp. 92–93),* famed for its collection of Impressionist paintings; and the Old Water Tower, the only public structure to survive the Great Fire of 1871. Adjacent to this quaint, fortress-like edifice is Water Tower Place, a gleaming glass-and-steel complex that

includes elegant shops, restaurants, and a hotel.

Among Chicago's other attractions are the very fine Shedd Aquarium, the Adler Planetarium, the Field Museum of Natural History, and Wrigley Field, home of the Chicago Cubs. The city also boasts the Chicago White Sox, as well as football, basketball, and hockey teams.

The Merchandise Mart, purchased by Joseph P. Kennedy in the 1930s, is the second largest single-story building in the world, housing more than 800 offices and showrooms.

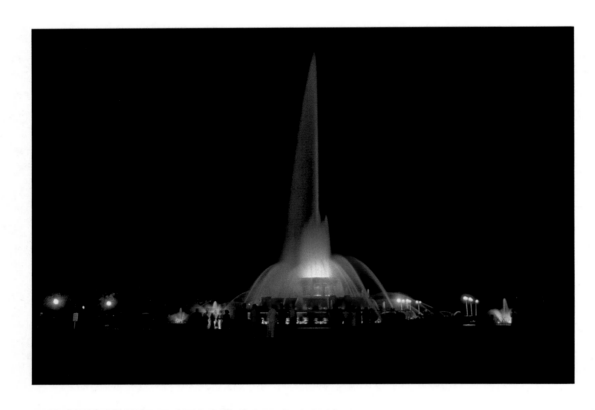

Grant Park's Buckingham Fountain, famed for its colorful light displays, is modeled after a Versailles waterworks.

(Opposite) Defiantly confronting the glass and steel giants around it, the Old Water Tower, built in 1868, is one of the few survivors of the Great Chicago Fire.

Soaring to a height of 1,454 feet, the Sears Tower, completed in 1974, is the world's tallest building.

The Museum of Science and Industry

The Museum of Science and Industry in Chicago's Jackson Park invites visitors to participate in many of its 2,000 exhibits. Founded in 1933, it was one of the first museums in the country to pioneer the use of "hands-on" displays to make science and technology easy to understand and fun to explore.

Spanning nearly 15 acres in what was once the Palace of Fine Arts of the 1893 World's Columbian Exposition, the museum includes a genuine German World War II submarine, a re-creation of a working coal mine, and a typical small-town Main Street at the turn of the century. There are also displays that explain such diverse subjects as the physiology of the brain, superconductivity, and the ways of managing urban waste. On a more fanciful note, the museum also houses Colleen Moore's celebrated doll house, along with full-scale vintage airplanes, trains, and automobiles.

The Henry Crown Space Center—the museum's first major expansion in 53 years—opened in July 1986. It displays such artifacts as the Aurora 7 Mercury spacecraft and Apollo 8, the first spacecraft to orbit the moon. Here too is an Omnimax Theater, with a screen 76 feet in diameter. Its films cover not only space flight, but also subjects pertaining to nature and ecology.

(Above) One of the museum's most popular exhibits is a 16-foot high fiberglass reproduction of a human heart. Initially installed in 1952, it was completely refurbished and reopened in 1988.

(Left) Since 1933, visitors have journeyed 50 feet below ground to view the museum's authentic reproduction of a southern Illinois coal mine.

Housed in a remnant of the 1893 World's
Columbian Exposition, the museum
features over 2,000 exhibits, many of which
offer "hands-on" opportunities.

The Art Institute of Chicago

(Opposite) Guarding the Art Institute's classical-Renaissance facade are two lions, one on the prowl with his tail out and one in defiance with his tail curved down. They are beloved symbols of Chicago.

Founded in 1879, the Art Institute of Chicago is home to one of the world's largest collections of French Impressionist and Post-impressionist paintings. Its extensive holdings also include other European and American works, medieval sculpture, near Eastern and Oriental pieces, primitive art, arms and armor, and prints.

Among the famous works to be found here are George Seurat's *Sunday on the Island of La Grande Jatte,* Henri de Toulouse-Lautrec's *At the Moulin Rouge,* Edward Hopper's *Nighthawks,* El Greco's *Assumption of the Virgin,* and perhaps the most familiar work of all, Grant Wood's *American Gothic.* Here too are the Thorne miniature rooms, which reproduce interiors from the 16th to the 20th centuries at a scale of one inch to one foot; and a reconstruction of archi-

tect Louis Sullivan's Trading Room from the Chicago Stock Exchange.

The museum is an outgrowth of the Chicago Academy of Design. Located downtown near Lake Michigan, it also houses the very fine School of the Art Institute and the Goodman Theater, a regional theater company with its own 633-seat auditorium.

In September 1988, the museum opened a new 128,000-square-foot wing designed by Thomas Beeby to showcase its collection of 20th-century American paintings and sculpture, and European decorative arts.

The museum is world-renowed for its Impressionist collection, including George Seurat's *Sunday Afternoon on the Island of La Grande Jatte (center).*

Far from the log cabin with which Lincoln is associated, this Greek revival home, acquired by Lincoln in 1839, was appropriate for a rising Illinois attorney.

The parlor, as it appeared in about 1860, was suitable for entertaining, as well as everyday life in a household with three growing boys.

Abraham Lincoln Home and Tomb

About a mile and a half from Lincoln's home is his tomb, designed and sculpted by Larkin Mead and dedicated in 1874.

The only home that Abraham Lincoln would ever own sits not far from the state capitol in Springfield, Illinois. Purchased in 1839 by the future president and his wife, Mary Todd Lincoln, for $1,200 cash and a small lot worth $300, the modest frame house saw Lincoln rise from an obscure circuit-riding lawyer to a United States congressman to the highest office in the land. Since he was still struggling when the one-and-a-half-story, Greek revival-style house was purchased, Lincoln himself chopped wood, carried water, and milked the cow when he was not covering his 12,000-square-mile circuit.

In the 1850s, Mary Todd Lincoln oversaw expansion of the home to two stories to accommodate the growing family; by then there were three sons (a fourth had died). In 1860, nominated for the presidency, Lincoln campaigned from his doorstep; victorious, he helped pack the household, roped the trunks, and wrote on their labels, "A. Lincoln, White House, Washington, D.C." Unfortunately, much of the family furniture, which was sold at the time of his election, was destroyed in the Great Chicago Fire of 1871.

Assassinated in Washington, D.C., in April 1865, Lincoln's body was returned to Springfield to be buried in Oak Ridge Cemetery; his grave is marked by an obelisk and a bronze bust, its nose worn shiny from the touch of generations of schoolchildren. Both the tomb, where his wife and three sons are also buried, and the home, declared a National Historic Site in 1971, are open to the public.

The Gateway Arch

The Gateway Arch, the centerpiece of St. Louis' historic riverfront, commemorates the city's role in America's western migration.

The soaring symbol of the nation's westward migration, the Gateway Arch stands on the 91-acre plaza of the Jefferson National Expansion Memorial which fronts the Mississippi River in St. Louis, Missouri.

Dedicated in 1968, the gleaming arch is 630 feet high with triangular legs that are 54 feet wide on each side. Designed by architect Eero Saarinen, the arch required exquisitely sophisticated engineering to execute; a deviation of any amount between the bases of the legs could have resulted in the monument's failure to meet perfectly at the zenith.

Visitors can reach an observation area at the top by riding one of the circular capsules that travel sideways up one leg and down the other. On windy days, one can feel the arch sway slightly. But don't worry. It's designed to withstand winds of 150 miles an hour and is engineered to never deflect more than 18 inches.

At the base is an underground visitor's center and the Museum of Westward Ex-pansion, where exhibits on the people and events of 19th-century America may be seen, along with films about the western migration, St. Louis, and the construction of the arch. Nearby are the arch's historic companions, the Old Cathedral, a house of worship since 1834, and the Old Courthouse, where Dred Scott's lawyer first pleaded for his freedom from slavery in 1847.

96

The Truman Home and Library

President Truman lived in this late-19th-century Victorian with his wife Bess from 1919 until his death in 1972.

Harry S Truman is buried on the grounds of the Truman Library, which houses memorabilia and papers covering his life and presidency.

The house that was the focus of Harry S Truman's affections was not the White House, which he called the "Great White Jail," but a white frame house in Independence, Missouri, 12 miles east of Kansas City. It was the family home of his wife, Bess, since 1867. When she and Harry married in 1919, they moved into the 14-room Victorian, its wraparound porch supported by carpenter gothic posts and its broad eaves by decorative brackets. The couple shared the home with Bess' grandmother and mother; the Trumans' daughter, Margaret, was born there in 1924.

During Truman's presidency, the house at 219 North Delaware Street became the "Summer White House." Here, Truman addressed the nation by radio on the eve of his upset election in 1948 and learned of the invasion of South Korea in 1950. Saying "I prefer my life in Missouri and I prefer to live the way I do," Truman chose not to run for a third term and returned to Independence. He and Bess made improvements to the house, and he took daily walks and helped organize his presidential library, also in Independence.

Visitors to the home will see the living room where the Trumans entertained guests; the music room, with the grand piano that they gave their daughter; the library, with its large book collection (Truman was an avid reader); the formal dining room where the evening meal was always eaten; and, by contrast, the homey kitchen where the couple ate breakfast and lunch. In the hallway on a bentwood rack are Truman's trademark hat and canes, which accompanied him on those early-morning strolls around the city he loved.

The Mark Twain Boyhood Home

The Hannibal, Missouri, house in which author and humorist Mark Twain lived as a child, figured in his classic tale, *The Adventures of Tom Sawyer*. Twain, whose real name was Samuel Langhorne Clemens, moved to Hannibal with his family when he was four years old. The exact age of the house, a simple frame dwelling, is unknown, although Twain wrote in his autobiography that his father, John Marshall Clemens, built it in 1844. It was dedicated as the Mark Twain Boyhood Home in 1912.

Next to the house is the Mark Twain Museum, which opened in 1937. It has an eclectic collection of Twain memorabilia: the desk at which Clemens wrote *Tom Sawyer,* his favorite typewriter, one of his white suits, 16 Norman Rockwell paintings depicting scenes from *Tom Sawyer* and *Huckleberry Finn,* correspondence, pictures of steamboats Twain piloted on the Mississippi, first-edition copies of his books, and the cap and gown he wore to receive a degree from Oxford University.

Nearby is the restored law office in which Twain's father held court as justice of the peace. The front room has been refurbished as a courtroom from Hannibal's early days, and the back re-creates the scene in *The Innocents Abroad,* in which Twain finds a body in his father's office. Also on view is the Pilaster House, into which the Clemens family moved in 1846 when financial difficulties forced the sale of their home. The first floor houses an early drug store, and the second is furnished with period pieces. And at Cardiff Hill nearby stands a sculpture of Tom and Huck dedicated in 1926.

A statue of Samuel Clemens — Mark Twain — stands in Riverview Park, about a mile from his boyhood home. The sculptor is Frederick Hibbard.

Around the corner from Twain's home is Hibbard's tribute to Tom Sawyer and Huckleberry Finn, believed to be the first statue in the United States representing literary figures.

The home of Twain's youth served as the model for Aunt Polly's house in *Tom Sawyer*, and the adjacent fence was the backdrop for the book's white-washing scene.

Henry Ford Museum & Greenfield Village

"When we are through, we shall have reproduced American life as lived," said inventor and industrialist Henry Ford of his plans for an historical complex near Dearborn, Michigan. The result, the Henry Ford Museum & Greenfield Village, founded in 1929, focuses on the United States from 1800 to 1950, the era in which America was transformed from a rural to an industrial society.

The museum's 12 acres of exhibits include such tools and products as a 600-ton coal-burning locomotive; a 1925 Fokker Trimotor, the first plane to fly over the North Pole; and a 1938 Massey-Harris combine, one of the first to be self-propelled. In a permanent exhibit, "The Automobile in American Life," more than 100 cars are on display, along with such related artifacts as a 1946 diner, a 1940s Texaco service station, an early 1960s Holiday Inn guest room, and a drive-in movie theater.

In the 81-acre village, guests can visit more than 80 buildings, many moved by Ford from their original sites. Among them is the boyhood farm-home of tire pioneer Harvey S. Firestone, set on seven acres; the farmhouse where Ford was born and raised; the laboratory of Thomas Edison, site of more than 400 inventions; the bicycle shop where Orville and Wilbur Wright built their first airplane; and the house where Noah Webster wrote his dictionary. Other attractions that dramatize the techno-logical changes in America include an operating sawmill, a pottery shop, a glassmaking plant, a print shop, and a machine shop.

A steam-powered locomotive takes visitors on a scenic journey around the perimeter of Greenfield Village's 81 acres.

(Opposite) An exact replica of Independence Hall's facade *(see p. 32)* gives entrance to the Henry Ford Museum, a 12-acre celebration of American technology and social history.

(Left) A major exhibit in the Henry Ford Museum, "The Automobile in American Life," traces the evolution of the car and the culture it has inspired.

(Below) In Greenfield Village's Suwanee Park, visitors can enjoy a relaxing cruise aboard an old paddlewheeler.

The French Quarter

In New Orleans, they call it the "Vieux Carré" (pronounced "view ka-ray"), which means "old square," and the French Quarter is just that—the old city of New Orleans founded by Creole settlers in 1718. To visitors, it is the home of jazz, mint juleps in hurricane glasses, and the annual carnival called Mardi Gras.

The heart of the original colony, the Place d'Armes, or parade grounds, is now called Jackson Square. Appropriately, it centers around a statue of Andrew Jackson and is a magnet for artists, mimes, musicians, and sightseers. Dominating the square is St. Louis Cathedral, the country's oldest, built in 1794.

Across the square is the French market, once an Indian trading post, which has occupied the site for two centuries and is now famous for its chicory coffee and beignets (a square type of doughnut). Nearby, the Moon Walk offers a block-long promenade to the river. In the hotel and commercial area, narrow streets are lined with pastel buildings, some no higher than three stories, and many garnished with lacy ironwork. Some are private residences, but many house shops, inns, and restaurants. Visitors are invariably drawn to Bourbon Street, a bemusing combination of the chic and the seedy, with hotels, jazz clubs, restaurants, and topless and bottomless bars. Antique shoppers seek out Royal and Magazine Streets, and jazz buffs flock to Preservation Hall, a tiny space with wood floor and benches, where traditional New Orleans music is played by the very best.

The cornerstone of the French Quarter is Jackson Square which houses St. Louis Cathedral *(center),* built in 1794.

106

(*Opposite*) New Orleans Creoles combined Spanish and French architectural influences to create a distinctive and charming style.

For afficionados of Dixieland jazz, nothing compares to the "no frills" atmosphere of Preservation Hall.

There are those who believe that New Orleans isn't New Orleans without a mint julip in a hurricane glass at Pat O'Brien's club.

Gilley's

To Texans, Gilley's in Pasadena, just east of Houston, has been a legend since owner and former welder Sherman Cryer opened the club in 1971 with Mickey Gilley and the Bayou City Beats as the major draw. The rest of America discovered the giant indoor "playground" for adults in 1980 when it played a prominent role in the movie *Urban Cowboy* starring John Travolta.

The biggest honkeytonk in Texas—in fact, it bills itself as the largest nightclub in the world—Gilley's Club is known for country-western music; for its regular patrons, the Gilleyrats; for its wraparound double bar; for its typical barroom games (pool, pinball, and video); and for its not-so-typical tests of strength (punching-bag, bullhorn-squeeze, and soccer-kick machines). But it may be best known for the awesome machine known as the "Bull," a motor-driven, three-horsepower mechanical bucking bovine, surrounded by mattresses and adorned with a sign: "Ride the Bull at Your Own Risk." As those in the know will confirm, the Bull nearly always wins.

Gilley's is a place where patrons favor western gear, where the *real* cowboys and cowgirls can be told by the quality of their feather-bedecked hats, where dancing is called "kickin'" and the favorite steps are the "Cotton-Eyed Joe" and the "Texas Two-Step." Above all, it's a place where would-be rodeo kings and queens can meet.

Through recent additions, Gilley's now also includes a recording studio, restaurant, western clothing store, and a next-door arena where rodeos are held each weekend.

Gilley's gained worldwide attention as the backdrop for the 1980 movie, *Urban Cowboy,* starring John Travolta.

Contemporary cowboys pit their strength against electronic punching machines in one of the club's more unusual recreational activities.

The Astrodome

When it opened in 1965, the Astrodome in Houston, Texas, was called the "eighth wonder of the world." Reportedly inspired by the Roman Coliseum, it was the world's largest clear-span building. It featured a computer-operated air-conditioning system that kept its dome at a constant temperature of 72 degrees and provided a breeze of one mile an hour blowing in each direction. Its four-story video scoreboard required a producer and six technicians to operate. And, perhaps, most impressively, its 208-foot-high translucent roof was tall enough to house an 18-story building.

Today the domed stadium, which seats up to 62,000 people, is home to two professional sports teams—the football Houston Oilers and the baseball Houston Astros—and also plays host to a variety of activities, from the Houston Livestock Show and Rodeo to rock concerts.

The Astrodome is the focal point of Astrodomain, an entertainment complex that includes Astrohall, an exhibition center, and Astroworld, a Six Flags theme park on 75 acres with more than 100 rides, shows, and attractions. Its 12 theme areas range from "Alpine Valley" to "Coney Island" and "Bugs Bunny's Enchanted Kingdom," and the park features five roller coasters, including the "Texas Cyclone," and the Astro-needle sightseeing tower.

The Astrodome, the first large-scale covered stadium, was called "the eighth wonder of the world" when it opened in 1965.

Six Flags Over Texas

Six Flags Over Texas, a family entertainment center on 200 acres of land in Arlington, Texas, between Dallas and Fort Worth, was the second modern theme park in the United States (after Disneyland). Since it opened in 1961, it has become the state's top tourist attraction. The park's name is drawn from Texas history—Texas has flown six flags: as a territory of Spain, France, and Mexico; as an independent republic; as a part of the Confederacy; and as the Lone Star State. A section of the park is devoted to each period of its history.

The park offers more than 100 thrill rides. Among them are three roller coasters: the "Shock Wave," billed as the longest, tallest, fastest double-loop roller coaster in the world; the "Runaway Train Mine," designed to give passengers the feeling of riding in an out-of-control mining-ore train; and "Judge Roy Scream," an old-fashioned roller coaster covering eight miles. Free-fall rides include the "Texas Cliffhanger," in which gondolas speed down the side of a 128-foot tower, and the "Texas Chute-Out," a 200-foot parachute drop. Water rides include 'Splashwater Falls," in which boats plunge over a five-story waterfall; "Roaring Rapids," which recalls a white-water raft trip; and two log flumes.

Other attractions are a special section for children, "Looney Tunes Land"; the 300-foot "Oil Derrick," from which visitors can see the skylines of the two nearby cities; and the "Silver Star Carousel," a vintage 1925 machine with 66 hand-carved horses, requiring 30,000 hours of restoration work. In the Southern Palace, five hours of musical revues are presented daily, and top-name entertainers perform in the 10,000-seat Music Mill Amphitheater.

(Opposite) Two of Six Flags' most popular attractions are the "Judge Roy Scream," a roller coaster stretching across eight miles *(foreground)*, and the "Texas Chute Out," a 17-story parachute drop *(rear)*.

Bugs Bunny and his friends preside over Looney Toons Land, a special section of the park designed for smaller children.

(*Right*) The undulating lights of the "Judge Roy Scream" create an arresting nighttime view of the 200-acre theme park.

(*Below*) In Looney Toons Land, toddlers can dive into a pen filled with soft plastic balls. Only those under 54 inches are admitted.

(*Bottom*) Splashwater Falls carries passengers up five stories and plunges them over a waterfall into the lake below.

The Alamo

Few events in America's history have stirred the popular imagination more than the 1836 martyrdom of Davey Crockett, Jim Bowie, and the 181 other freedom fighters who stood against the powerful Mexican army of Santa Anna in an effort to obtain Texas' independence. The name of the battle site, the Alamo, became a rallying cry that every schoolchild still knows, and its remnants are Texas' most popular historic attraction.

First established as the Mission San Antonio de Valero at another location in 1718, the stone structure was moved to its present site in the 1720s; all that remains today are the barracks and the chapel, in which the defenders of the mission-fort barricaded themselves.

The battle of the Alamo began after a group of Texas colonists—called Texians—rebelled and captured San Antonio. Santa Anna, Mexico's president, took command of his country's army and marched to the settlement, where fewer than 200 rebels remained. Hoping for reinforcements, the commanders of the Texians ordered their troops into the walled chapel and waited. But only 32 more men arrived to face a Mexican force of 4,000. The siege, which had lasted 13 days, was over in hours, but the cry "Remember the Alamo!" inspired the rebels, who ultimately defeated Santa Anna's forces at the Battle of San Jacinto.

The Alamo grounds today include a garden and museum that offers slide shows and guided tours.

"Remember the Alamo!"—the rallying cry during Texas' War of Independence—helped make this church fortress one of America's most hallowed landmarks.

115

Mount Rushmore

From the rock of Mount Rushmore, the colossal heads of four American presidents dominate the surrounding terrain in the Black Hills National Forest, 25 miles southwest of Rapid City, South Dakota. As a group, the figures symbolize the first 150 years of United States history; individually, they represent the nation's ideals: George Washington, the struggle for independence; Thomas Jefferson, the concept of representative government; Abraham Lincoln, equality and union; and Theodore Roosevelt, the United States as a world leader.

The faces were not carved but "engineered." Their rough outlines were blasted with dynamite from the granite cap of the 6,000-foot mountain, and workers in suspended seats used jackhammers, drills, and hammers to remove excess stone. An estimated 450,000 tons of rock were subtracted. Work began in 1927 on the day that Mount Rushmore officially was dedicated a national memorial, but the sculpture was not completed until 1941. It actually took only six and a half years to create the figures; delays were caused by lack of funds and bad weather.

Originally supported by private donations, the sculpture was eventually financed by the federal government, which paid $836,000 of the $900,000 total. The sculptor, John Gutzon de la Mothe Borglum, died before the work was completed; his son, Lincoln, continued the project until funds were exhausted.

A visitor's center is open year-round; from Memorial Day to Labor Day, an evening sculpture-lighting program is presented in an amphitheater.

This unusual view of the monument overlooks Washington's head to show a detail of Jefferson's profile and, beyond that, the bust of Lincoln.

For his monumental sculpture, begun in 1927, Gutzon Borglum chose to portray the four U.S. presidents that to him were most representative of the nation's ideals: George Washington, Thomas Jefferson, Abraham Lincoln, and Theodore Roosevelt.

The West

The spectacular terraces of Mammoth Hot
Springs are formed by travertine (calcium
carbonate) which is deposited daily.

(Previous pages) The Space Needle, construc-
ted for the 1962 World's Fair, remains a
towering symbol of Seattle.

Yellowstone National Park

Segments of three states—western Wyoming, eastern Idaho, and southern Montana—were combined in 1872 to form Yellowstone, the world's first national park. Today, its 142-mile road system, shaped like a figure eight, enables visitors to view the awe-inspiring results of two million years of volcanic activity: geysers, hot springs, fumaroles, and mud pots.

The park's most popular attraction is Old Faithful, the world's best-known geyser, which erupts every 76 minutes on average. Fifty-one miles north of Old Faithful is Mammoth Hot Springs, where spectacular terraces are formed from daily deposits of travertine. The route between these sites provides a scenic journey through pristine forests of lodgepole pine and other geyser basins. The park also features the Grand Canyon of the Yellowstone River, which is home to grizzly bears, pronghorn antelope, mule deer, and elk, and the beautiful but frigid Yellowstone Lake. At 20 miles long and 14 miles wide, it is the largest mountain lake in North America.

North of Yellowstone Lake is Hayden Valley, which plays host to a wide range of waterfowl, including white pelicans and trumpeter swans and to mammals, such as bison and moose. Also in the north are petrified redwoods, some still upright, covering hundreds of square miles.

For hikers, the back country offers thousands of miles of trails while those interested in history and geology may wish to explore the exhibits throughout the park that describe Yellowstone's rich past. Boating, fishing, and camping are allowed but require park permits.

(*Left*) Old Faithful, the world's best-known geyser, erupts every 76 minutes on average.

(*Following pages*) Lake Yellowstone, North America's largest mountain lake, offers a placid alternative to the park's more volatile attractions.

The Mormon Tabernacle

The Mormon Tabernacle is part of Temple Square, a 10-acre city block that is the historic heart of Salt Lake City, Utah, and the symbolic heart of the Mormon Church (or the Church of Jesus Christ of Latter-Day Saints, as it is officially known). Completed in 1867, the Tabernacle is an oval building spanned by a domed roof resting on 44 sandstone pillars. It is 250 feet long, 150 feet wide, and 80 feet high and is renowned for its fine acoustics; one literally can hear a pin drop from 200 feet away. A major attraction is the organ, which is among the finest in the world, but the facility is best known as the home of the Mormon Tabernacle Choir. Both choir and organ date to the church's pioneer days; the former was founded by the Mormon's leader, Brigham Young; the latter was built of pine hauled 300 miles by ox-drawn wagon and operated by hand-pumped bellows (long since replaced by electricity). Some of its first painstakingly shaped pipes can still be found among the more than 11,000 now in use. Radio and television broadcasts since 1929 have brought both the instrument and the choir of 325 volunteers world acclaim.

Other buildings in Temple Square include the famed Salt Lake Temple, a soaring edifice which took 40 years to complete; the Assembly Hall, a place of public worship completed in 1882; and the Old House, a log cabin built in the 1840s, shortly after the Mormon pioneers arrived in Utah seeking refuge from religious persecution. Contemporary buildings include a visitor's center with displays and films about the church's history and doctrine, and a museum with relics of the early West. The church estimates that two million people visit Temple Square annually.

(Top) The acclaimed Tabernacle organ has 11,623 pipes, some of which date to the instrument's 19th-century creation.

(Above) The Mormon Tabernacle, completed when Salt Lake City was an isolated pioneer community, features a massive domed roof designed by a bridge builder, Henry Grow.

The Las Vegas Strip is home to big-name entertainers and to mammoth luxury hotels, such as Caesar's Palace (*left*) and the Flamingo (*right*).

Las Vegas

There is not one Las Vegas but two: downtown, also known as "Glitter Gulch"; and the newer, more expensive area, known as the "Strip." Along the four-block downtown section are such big-name establishments as the Golden Nugget Hotel, where entertainers Frank Sinatra and Willie Nelson perform, and Binion's Horseshoe, known as the *real* gamblers' favorite casino because there is virtually no betting limit. Several miles away is the Strip, location of prominent

performers and plush hotels—the MGM Grand, Caesar's Palace, and the Tropicana among them. Here also is the Flamingo Hotel, built by mobster Benjamin "Bugsy" Siegel just after World War II and named for his girlfriend, Virginia "Flamingo" Hill. A block off the Strip is the Las Vegas Hilton, the largest luxury resort hotel in the world with more than 3,000 rooms.

To call these hotels plush is perhaps to redefine the word. The most expensive suites can cost as much as $2,500 a day; lobbies and casinos are filled with such sights as Caesar's Palace's 20-foot-high copy of Michelangelo's *David,* carved in

marble from the same quarry as the original. The MGM Grand has 2,832 rooms and suites, two full-size showrooms, 40 shops, seven restaurants, a movie theater, and, of course, a casino.

Beyond gambling and nightclub shows, the desert resort town also offers a host of outdoor recreational activities, including golf on superb courses and horseback riding.

Las Vegas may not have invented the "show girl" but it has certainly kept the tradition alive.

In downtown Las Vegas there are more than a dozen major hotels within four blocks, creating the most brightly lit area in the world.

Hoover Dam

The dam that tamed the tumbling Colorado River—once considered America's most dangerous—rears skyward in the Black Canyon linking Arizona and Nevada. At 726 feet from foundation to crest, and with towers rising 40 feet higher, Hoover Dam is the tallest concrete dam in the western hemisphere.

This stunning engineering achievement, about 30 miles southeast of Las Vegas, weighs about 7 million tons and is 660 feet thick at its base. It produces an average of 3.5 billion kilowatt hours of electrical energy each year, serving the needs of the Southwest. It also provides flood control and helps irrigate up to 1.5 million acres of land in the arid southwestern United States and in Mexico.

An average of 3,500 men worked on the dam from 1931 to 1936; 96 of them died. Before construction could begin, an entire town—Boulder City, Nevada—had to be created to house employees. In addition, a 7-mile-long highway was built, more than 32 miles of railway tracks were laid, and 222 miles of transmission lines were strung. Nearly 4.4 million cubic yards of concrete were required to build the dam, enough to pave a two-lane highway from New York City to San Francisco.

Integral to the project was the creation of Lake Mead, the longest artificial reservoir in the United States. The Lake Mead National Recreation Area offers sightseeing, camping, boating, fishing, and swimming.

A night view of Hoover Dam looking downstream from Lake Mead. The four fluted towers extend several hundred feet below the surface where they carry water to the dam's hydroelectric generating units.

Monument Valley

In the 1860s, when the U.S. Cavalry under famed scout Christopher "Kit" Carson was rounding up Indians for forced relocation, Navajo Chief Hoskinnini blocked the only trail up the mesa on which his 40 people were trapped, successfully evaded capture, and settled in what became known as Monument Valley.

The Navajo's "hogans" (eight-sided homes of logs and mud) can still be found nestled among the rocks and juniper, where flocks of sheep graze on the sparse vegetation. Descendants of the original tribe live here today and the mesa still bears Hoskinnini's name. Some of the valley's imposing red sandstone formations are named for others who braved this arid land. Merrick Butte, for example, recalls a silver prospector killed there. Formations are also named for the shapes they evoke—the Mittens, Elephant Butte, Camel Butte, and the Three Sisters. Among the tallest is Agathla Peak, or El Capitan, a volcanic neck whose spire reaches 1,255 feet above its base.

This remote spot, which covers parts of Utah and Arizona, is familiar to virtually anyone who has seen a western movie for it has served as the backdrop for dozens of films, including those of director John Ford. Its spectacular sights are best seen on guided tours in four-wheel-drive vehicles; headquarters for tours is Goulding's Trading Post Lodge, built originally to house filmmakers and their crews.

The relatively young and rugged terrain of the American West is dramatically apparent in Monument Valley, site of innumerable Hollywood westerns.

129

London Bridge

Built in 1831, the stone bridge known as London Bridge was the fourth to span London's Thames River in 2,000 years; incorporated into it were sections of its predecessor, built 600 years earlier. By the mid-1960s, the 928-foot long, two-lane bridge could no longer accommodate the flow of commuter traffic into the city's core, and, in 1968, the British government sold it for $2,460,000 to the highest bidder, Robert McCulloch, an industrialist developer who moved it to his resort community, Lake Havasu City, Arizona.

Its reconstruction, at a cost of $7.5 million, has been called one of the world's great engineering feats. More than 10,000 tons of granite had to be dismantled in England, shipped through the Panama Canal to California, and brought to Arizona. There the thousands of pieces, each numbered, were rebuilt into their five arches over immense mounds of sand that conformed to the bridge's original profile. The lord mayor of London laid the cornerstone in September 1968, and the bridge, which crosses a channel of Lake Havasu, was dedicated in October 1971.

Lake Havasu, 45 miles long, is formed by the Parker Dam on the Colorado River. The planned community includes some light industry, but it primarily offers resort and recreational activities and related services. Below the bridge is a replica of an English village, and nearby is a medieval-theme shopping complex patterned on the fifth-century "Shambles" in York, England.

After serving the British for more than 130 years, London Bridge has found new life on the banks of Lake Havasu in Arizona.

Carlsbad Caverns

What is now the Guadelupe Mountains in southeastern New Mexico was once part of a 400-mile-long reef covered by an inland sea. Two hundred fifty million years later, Carlsbad Caverns, one of the world's largest caves, serves as a reminder of that prehistoric age. More than 20 miles of the cave have been explored since its rediscovery by settlers in the 1800s; it is now part of a national park that includes more than 70 smaller caves, a scenic drive through desert mountains, and 50 miles of primitive, back-country trails.

Two tours of the caverns are offered; one, three miles long, begins at the cave's natural entrance; the other, one-and-a-quarter miles long, starts with an elevator ride 755 feet down. The longer tour takes visitors 829 feet below the surface through the Main Corridor (with ceiling heights of more than 200 feet) and into four scenic chambers decorated with exquisite natural limestone formations. Both tours cover the 14-acre "Big Room." This cross-shaped enclosure is up to 1,800 feet long, 1,100 wide, and 255 high. Among its formations are the 62-foot-high Giant Dome, the caverns' biggest stalagmite, and the 42-foot-high Twin Domes. Other features are the crystalline Mirror Lake and a 140-foot-deep hole, the Bottomless Pit.

The caverns are sanctuary to about 300,000 Mexican free-tail bats, who depart the caves each evening to feast on insects. This exodus can be viewed from a special amphitheater during the months of spring, summer, and early fall. Their flight from the cave's natural entrance can take up to two-and-a-half hours.

(*Top*) It took 250 million years to create the exquisite natural limestone formations of Carlsbad Caverns, the world's third largest cave.

(*Above*) From the mouth of the cavern, visitors can walk 829 feet below ground where a magnificent subterranean world awaits.

The Grand Canyon

The Grand Canyon is arguably the most famous—and the best-loved—natural wonder in America. Certainly, at up to a mile deep and up to 18 miles wide, it is among the most spectacular. Just consider a few statistics: the canyon, from North Rim to South, averages 10 miles by air; to cross it by car takes 215 miles and five hours; curling through it for 277 miles is the Colorado River which, at a moderate speed, can carry boulders weighing a ton.

Visitors can see the canyon by driving along either rim. The North, a thousand feet higher than the South, is cooler and wetter and hosts a spruce-fir forest. Here, tourist services are available from Memorial Day to mid-October. On the South Rim, in Grand Canyon Village, is the park headquarters and a visitor's center where services are open all year. Here too are the Yavapai Museum, which offers exhibits on the canyon's geology, and the Tusayan Museum, which tells the history of the prehistoric people who made the Colorado Plateau and canyon their home.

Those who wish to go into the canyon may hike trails from either rim or take mule trips; one-day jaunts and overnight treks are offered. In addition to the road, the rims are connected by a trail whose suspension bridge over the river is wide enough to accommodate one person and a mule. For the truly adventuresome, river operators offer guided trips of up to three week's duration in oar-powered or motorized crafts. Sightseeing from small aircraft also is available.

There is simply no other place on earth like the Grand Canyon. At 277 miles long and up to 18 miles wide, it provides viewers with scenes of incomparable beauty.

No visit to the Grand Canyon is truly complete without a muletrip to the floor of the canyon. The round-trip journey typically takes two days.

The Petrified Forest and the Painted Desert

Once covered by a freshwater sea and locked in rock for thousands of years, the natural secrets of arid eastern Arizona are gloriously revealed in the Petrified Forest National Park and the adjacent Painted Desert Wilderness, located east of Flagstaff. The logs of the "forest," hardened by silica deposits, are about 200 million years old while traces of human habitation date back 2,000 years.

Eight lookout points along a 27-mile scenic drive afford views of the desert, whose colors are created by bands of white sandstone, red irons, and darker carbon and clay. There are stops at such

natural formations as the Tepees, where badlands have been eroded into awesome sculptures; Blue Mesa, where pedestal petrified logs cap soft clay; and Crystal Forest, where log hollows once held quartz and amethyst crystals.

Near Chinde Point, the world's oldest dinosaur skeleton, dating back 225 million years, was found in 1985. Nicknamed "Gertie," the plant-eating plateosaur, about the size of a German shepherd, was an ancestor of the giant brontosaurs. In the Painted Desert Inn Museum, paleontological exhibits feature skeletal reconstructions of other large reptiles that also inhabited Arizona in prehistoric times. The Rainbow Forest Museum has exhibits on petrified wood

and the area's geological and human history. At the Puerco Indian Ruins, excavated and partially restored rooms attest to habitation before 1400, and, through telescopes, visitors can see Newspaper Rock, a huge sandstone block covered with petroglyphs.

In the Painted Desert, nature's palette is richly apparent as bands of color emerge from the desert's eroded shale, sandstone, and marl.

The logs of the Petrified Forest, hardened by silica deposits, lie freely on the park's surface.

Tiger River, a three-acre replica of a rain forest, exemplifies the zoo's method of exhibiting animals in a naturalistic environment.

San Diego Zoo

Starting with a few specimens left in Balboa Park at the close of the Panama-California International Exposition in 1916, the San Diego Zoo has grown to 3,500 animals of 800 species in a 100-acre tropical garden. The zoo has gained worldwide acclaim for its preferred method of exhibiting its inhabitants in barless, moated enclosures that resemble the animals' natural homes. In addition to such favorites as lions, tigers, elephants, and giraffes, there are rare and exotic species including koalas, kiwis, Przewalski's horses, and pygmy chimpanzees. A special exhibit area, Tiger River is a three-acre replica of a rain forest that mixes a wide range of animals and plants from the same bioclimatic zone, among them crocodiles and kingfishers, fishing cats and cattails, tigers and tapirs, pythons and pheasants. The children's zoo, built to the scale of an average four-year-old, features young animals, some of which can be petted; an egg-hatching incubator; and a nursery where infant mammals are bottle-fed and diapered.

Visitors can tour the zoo in a three-mile, 40-minute bus ride that roams through "canyons" and "mesas," or take the Skyfari aerial tram for a bird's-eye view of reptiles, monkeys, great apes, sealions, and the denizens of the Horn and Hoof Mesa. The zoo also offers a two-hour behind-the-scenes guided tour that explains how animals are fed, housed, and medically cared for.

This koala, one of the few on display outside of Australia, apparently prefers posing for the camera to watching a double-decker bus pass by.

These tin foil barb enjoy Fresh Water
Aquarium, which is also home to sting rays,
piranhas, and electric eel.

"The Penguin Encounter," an authentic
re-creation of Antarctica, houses these
emperor penguin and six related species.

Sea World

Since it opened in 1964 with a few dolphins, sea lions, and waterfowl, Sea World in San Diego, California, has grown to a 135-acre aquatic park with 200 marine animals, more than 10,000 fish, 5,000 invertebrates, and 1,600 birds.

Sea World is an entertainment bonanza with as many as nine shows in performance during the summer months. The most famous of these features three adult killer whales—including the world-renowned Shamu—and a baby, born in 1988. Other shows include a pearl-diving demonstration in a re-created Japanese village; an indoor extravaganza featuring fountains of water with lights, lasers, and music; "Pirates of Pinniped" which showcases sea lions, otters, and walruses; and "City Streets," a musical variety show celebrating urban America.

Beyond the lavish entertainments and demonstrations, Sea World also offers dozens of exhibits. Among the most popular is the Penguin Encounter, which carries visitors along a moving 100-foot viewing platform for a glimpse of an authentic re-creation of Antarctica. Behind its Plexiglas walls, more than 400 penguins are on display. Another popular attraction is the Shark Exhibit, a 400,000 gallon tank with a dozen sharks representing a variety of species. There is also a whale and dolphin petting pool and a pool where visitors can feed sea lions and walruses.

Sea World conducts extensive research activities, some of which may be seen by visitors on behind-the-scenes tours. Breeding programs in San Diego and at related parks in Ohio, Florida, and Texas have produced more than 1,000 penguins, 40 bottlenose dolphins, 100 California sea lions, and numerous rare waterfowl.

Leaping dolphins and black whales are among the aquatic park's celebrated entertainers.

The Spruce Goose, the largest airplane ever built, was airborne only once, for a test flight in 1947, piloted by Howard Hughes.

The Queen Mary and The Spruce Goose

The largest ocean liner afloat and the largest airplane ever built share the billing in this entertainment complex at the port of Long Beach, California.

More than 1,000 feet long, the *Queen Mary* is considered the last of the great super liners. Visitors may take a self-guided tour through portions of the ship, whose 365 wood-paneled staterooms are now a hotel. The tour includes replicas of the original staterooms, crew quarters, the first-class drawing room, the engine room and the wheelhouse. There is also a Hall of Maritime Heritage with ship models and paintings, and a wedding chapel where about 600 marriage ceremonies are performed each year by the ship's captain.

Adjacent to the *Queen Mary* is Howard Hughes' massive flying boat, the Spruce Goose. This unique aircraft, with a wingspan of 320 feet, was airborne only once, for a test flight by Hughes in 1947. Despite its name, the plane, originally designed to transport World War II troops across the Atlantic, is made primarily of laminated birch. Visitors can board the eight-story-high craft to view the flight deck and the cargo bay (with room for 750 men or two 30-ton Sherman tanks).

Surrounding the Spruce Goose in a specially built hanger 415 feet in diameter are displays and audiovisual presentations about the plane's construction and test flight, and about its enigmatic creator. Near the exhibition areas is a group of shops and snack bars styled to resemble a 19th-century English village called "Londowntowne."

The last of the great ocean liners, the *Queen Mary,* now serves two roles—as hotel and as a visitor's attraction.

Disneyland

As a father raising young daughters, Walt Disney grew frustrated by the lack of places that provided entertainment for the whole family, places that adults as well as children could enjoy. Being Walt Disney, he decided to do something about it. He created Disneyland, a unique theme park in Anaheim, California. The Magic Kingdom, opened in 1955, became an immediate sensation and remains, more than 30 years later, one of the most popular places in America.

Visitors enter Disneyland through Main Street, U.S.A., a turn-of-the-century shopping district with gas lights, picturesque Victorian buildings, and a steam train. Beyond lie four enchanting "lands"—Fantasyland, Frontierland, Adventureland, and Tomorrowland. Directly ahead is Fantasyland, where rides center on such characters as Pinocchio, Snow White, and Peter Pan. Frontierland evokes the Wild West with a roller coaster that simulates a runaway mining car and giant paddlewheelers that explore "uncharted" waters. Adventureland features the famed "Jungle Cruise" and "Swiss Family Robinson" attractions, while Tomorrowland offers "Star Tours," based on the film *Star Wars,* and *Captain EO,* a Michael Jackson 3D movie. Tomorrowland is also the home of "Space Mountain," a roller coaster that rockets past galactic marvels inside a blackened interior.

In addition to the major "lands," New Orleans Square features the popular attractions, "Pirates of the Caribbean" and "The Haunted Mansion," while "Bear Country," now known as "Critter Country," offers a new ride, "Splash Mountain," with 100 robotic characters and a log flume that drops 52 feet.

One of Snow White's seven diminutive friends greets an even more diminutive guest.

The whirling cups and saucers of the Mad Tea Party create a rainbow of colors in one of the park's original rides, dating to July 1955.

At the entrance to Disneyland, a floral portrait of Mickey Mouse sets the stage for the many enchanting sights to come.

Los Angeles

(*Opposite*) Emblazoned across the side of the hill in letters 50 feet high is the name of the community that is synonymous with the movie industry. Originally the sign read "Hollywoodland" and promoted a real estate development.

Los Angeles is a visitor's paradise. It offers activities suited to every taste in a mild climate where the sun invariably shines. There are, of course, the beaches; the Pacific Ocean is only 15 miles away. Mountains, too, are within an hour's drive.

But it is Los Angeles' connection with the movies that gives the city its unique character. People flock to Hollywood to see the stars' foot- and handprints outside Mann's Chinese Theatre, and to follow the celebrity plaques embedded in cement along the Hollywood Walk of Fame. They cruise through Beverly Hills and Bel-Air, where plush estates house the rich and famous. And they enjoy shopping on Rodeo Drive which not only features elegant shops but also many celebrity customers.

Movies aside, the nation's second largest city boasts professional teams in every major sport, and horse racing at Santa Anita, one of the nation's best-known tracks. There is a zoo and observatory—both in Griffith park—and the Music Center, which is home to the Los Angeles Philharmonic, the Joffrey Ballet, and the Los Angeles Opera. Museums provide art lovers with a wide range of choices—from the new Museum of Contemporary Art downtown to the Huntington Hartford and Norton Simon Museums in Pasadena (featuring British art and an eclectic personal collection, respectively). There is also the J. Paul Getty Museum near Malibu, which offers antiquities, decorative arts, and paintings in a stunning facility modeled after an ancient Roman villa.

Rodeo Drive, in Beverly Hills entices visitors with its many elegant stores, including Van Cleef & Arpels (*right*) and Battaglia.

Since 1922, the 17,000-seat Hollywood Bowl has offered a series of summer concerts under the stars. Its superb band shell was designed by Frank Lloyd Wright.

Norma Talmadge started the tradition by accidentally stepping in cement at the opening of Grauman's Chinese Theatre. Today Mann's Chinese displays over 170 autographed hand- and footprints, including those of Bing Crosby.

Built for the 1932 Olympics and the center-piece of the 1984 games, the 92,000-seat Coliseum is home to the Los Angeles Raiders football team.

Visitors to the Entertainment Center watch
the filming of a commercial on the *Moulin
Rouge* set. Portions of Universal Studios
Hollywood are frequently used for actual
film work.

Universal Studios Hollywood

A trip through Universal Studios Hollywood is a journey through a hundred film fantasies as an open-air tram takes visitors through select portions of the studio's 420-acre motion-picture and television production facility between Hollywood and the San Fernando Valley. Along the way, they experience re-creations of classic movie special effects, the most spectacular of which is the "Big One," an earthquake measuring 8.3 on the Richter scale. The tram is also attacked by: evil alien Cylons from the televi-

sion series *Battlestar Galactica*; a 30-foot King Kong as he tries to demolish the Brooklyn Bridge; and the man-eating shark of *Jaws*. The tram also negotiates the collapsing bridge of television's *Bionic Woman*, drives through the middle of a 600-foot lake in a simulation of Cecil B. DeMille's parting of the Red Sea, and spins through an icy cavern in a tribute to Alfred Hitchcock.

Along the seven-hour tour, visitors pass through the studios' back lot, where they can see sets used in classic films and television shows past and present. In the Entertainment Center, there is a participation show based on *Star Trek* and special effects and stunt demonstrations called the *Miami Vice Spectacular, The Adventures of Conan,* and the *Western Stunt Show.* Other attractions include

Animal Actors Stage, where trainers work with their charges, and *Streets of the World,* which re-creates such famed movie sets as the Baker Street of Sherlock Holmes' adventures, Faber College from *Animal House,* and Mel's Diner of *American Graffiti.* In addition, special events are scheduled in a 2,300-seat open-air theater.

A highlight of the tour is a visit to Universal's vast back lot where visitors can view such well-known structures as the Cleaver home from *Leave It to Beaver,* the Victorian mansion in *Psycho,* and the town square in *Back to the Future.*

"Sherlock Holmes" and "Dr. Watson" chat amid the bustle of Baker Street, part of the elaborate "Street of the World" attraction.

The Jo Ann and Julian Ganz, Jr. Gallery features American 19th-century paintings, decorative arts, and sculpture, including Randolph Rogers' *Nydia, The Blind Flower Girl of Pompeii* (right).

(*Opposite*) Amid the 19th-century works in the B. Gerald Cantor Sculpture Garden, which opened in July 1988, are Rodin's *Large Torso of Falling Man* (foreground) and *Eve* (rear).

Los Angeles County Museum of Art

Founded in 1913 as part of the Los Angeles County Museum of History, Science, and Art, LACMA—as the museum affectionately is known—moved into its own three-building complex on Wilshire Boulevard in 1965. Rapidly outgrowing its 100,000 square feet, the museum, which is now the largest and most comprehensive in the western United States, opened a new three-floor building in 1986. The addition, the Robert O. Anderson Building, was designed in the colorful postmodern style by Holzman Pfeiffer Associates of New York. It features a 50-foot-square entrance portal in bands of glass block alternating with stone and sea-green tile, and a columned entry court illuminated by skylights. The building houses the museum's extensive collection of 20th-century art and large special exhibits, for which the museum is gaining considerable attention. Also new is the Pavilion for Japanese Art, which features a collection of more than 300 scroll paintings and screens.

The original galleries, built around a central atrium, display a permanent collection of paintings, sculptures, graphic arts, costumes, textiles, and decorative arts that extend from prehistoric times to the present. The museum also houses one of the Western world's largest assemblages of Indian, Nepalese, and Tibetan art, and offers film, lecture, and concert series.

Yosemite National Park

At Yosemite National Park, on the eastern flank of the Sierra Nevada Mountains north of Fresno, California, visitors can explore three distinct types of terrain at elevations that range from 2,000 to 13,000 feet about sea level.

The first level is Yosemite Valley, a glacier-carved canyon on the Merced River that includes some of the park's best-known features: El Capitan, Half Dome, and Cathedral Rocks. Often called the "incomparable valley," its floor is a mosaic of meadows, oak woods, and a conifer forest that abounds with wildlife, from monarch butterflies to mule deer to black bear. The visitor's center provides exhibits on Yosemite's natural and human history, and the Indian Cultural Museum and Village focus on the area's earliest inhabitants, the Ahwahneechee Indians.

On the second level is Mariposa Grove. Thirty-five miles south of the valley, it is the largest of the park's three sequoia groves and the site of the Grizzly Giant, believed to be the oldest of these ancient trees, at 2,700 years. Between Yosemite and Mariposa is the Wawona Hotel, built in 1875, and the Pioneer Yosemite History Center, a collection of relocated historic buildings and horse-drawn coaches.

The third level, 55 miles from Yosemite Valley, features the High Country and Tolumne Meadows, the largest subalpine meadow in the Sierras. At Tioga Pass, there are the contrasting vistas of peaks and meadows to the west and high desert to the east. In the back country, more than 750 miles of trails are open for activities from hiking to snowshoeing. Camping is permitted.

El Capitan, the largest exposed granite monolith in the world, is twice the height of the Rock of Gibraltar.

Yellowstone Falls, which reaches a level of 1,430 feet, is the highest waterfall in North America and the second highest in the world.

(Opposite) Half Dome, the largest rock in the region, is well known to photography lovers (along with many of Yosemite's other sites) through the silvery black and white images of Ansel Adams.

Often called "incomparable," Yosemite Valley's floor is a mosaic of meadows, oak wood, and a conifer forest that abounds with wildlife.

San Simeon

After Disneyland, the most popular attraction in California is the vast estate south of Carmel that newspaper publisher William Randolph Hearst spent more than 25 years creating. Officially called the Hearst San Simeon State Historical Monument, and generally known as San Simeon, it features an awesome collection of European treasures that leaves few visitors unimpresssed.

Work on the estate began in 1919 when Hearst engaged architect Julia Morgan to design a retreat for himself and the love of his life, actress Marian Davies. Situated on Enchantment Hill, the estate, which once covered 250,000 acres, includes three guest houses, a private zoo, an indoor pool, and an outdoor pool so lavish it was used in the movie *Spartacus.* But the principal attraction is Casa Grande, echoing the Spanish colonial style, and containing 100 rooms, including a billiard room, a theater, a library with 5,000 books and a collection of ancient Greek pottery, and Hearst's private suite, which occupies the entire third floor. Equal to the buildings are the grounds of the estate. During his lifetime, Hearst's greenhouses provided 650,000 to 700,000 plants each year.

Developed in part as a place to entertain guests, including Winston Churchill, Will Rogers, and Greta Garbo, Casa Grande was also designed to house many of Hearst's European art treasures—paintings, sculptures, and decorative arts dating from the 15th century. Many of these masterpieces may be seen on the different tours that cover the estate. Visitors are advised to book tours in advance, however, as they frequently sell out.

Rising from the Enchanted Hill are the majestic towers of Casa Grande, inspired by those of the cathedral Santa Maria la Mayor in Ronda, Spain.

The indoor pool is dazzling, with its combination of blue and gold tiles from Murano, Italy, alabaster lampstands, and classically inspired statues by Carlo Freter.

Perched on a hillside (and reinforced by concrete beams), the Neptune pool creates such a rich Greco-Roman atmosphere that it was used in the movie *Spartacus*.

San Francisco

San Francisco may well be the most beloved city in the United States. There is something about the mix of natural beauty (the hills, the bay, the fog), the Gold Rush–Barbary Coast heritage, and the anything-goes tolerance of its citizens that make the city irresistible.

Founded in 1776, San Francisco became a boomtown after the discovery of gold in 1848, but in 1906 the city was devastated by the most severe earthquake and fire in U.S. history. Seven hundred people were killed; most of the central city was destroyed. But San Francisco rebuilt itself and today, with nearly 800,000 residents, it is second only to New York in population density; all these people are tucked into 45½ very hilly square miles.

As a port, San Francisco has long attracted immigrants. Chinatown, for example, is the largest Chinese community outside Asia. With a population of about 100,000, it offers more than 100 restaurants, lively markets, and a historical society. Visitors can reach Chinatown by way of the city's famed cable cars, which were declared a National Historic Landmark in 1964. The cars also stop at Fisherman's Wharf, where seafood restaurants and take-away counters abound. Nearby are such posh malls as Ghiradelli Square, a former chocolate factory, and the Cannery, once a fruit-and-vegetable packing plant.

The carnival atmosphere of Fisherman's Wharf invites visitors to sample fine restaurants or snack at numerous seafood stalls. There are also specialty shops, souvenir stands, and novelty museums.

Among a host of other attractions are Alcatraz, the former federal penitentiary; the Exploratorium, a very popular "hands-on" science museum; and the California Palace of the Legion of Honor, the only museum in the United States devoted entirely to French art.

(Opposite) The cable cars, seen here directly above Fisherman's Wharf (with Alcatraz Island in the background), have been in active service since 1873 and were declared a National Landmark 91 years later.

Once home to America's most hardened criminals, the former federal penitentiary Alcatraz has been open to touring visitors since 1973.

San Franciscans call Lombard Street the crookedest street in the world, and anyone who has driven down it understands why.

The twin towers of the Golden Gate Bridge rise to a height of 746 feet above San Francisco Bay. The bridge was completed in 1937 at the then-staggering cost of $35 million.

(*Opposite*) The brightly ornamented buildings in Chinatown contain a wide array of imported goods and approximately 100 restaurants. The Chinese Historical Society of America is here as well.

The Space Needle

The Space Needle, symbol of the 1962 World's Fair, rises 605 feet above downtown Seattle, Washington. More than 25 years after completion, the futuristic tower is still compelling; its dramatic use of curves and its seemingly delicate sense of balance continue to please the eye.

Equally pleasing are the views from the tower's observation deck. Here, 518 feet above ground, a magnificent panorama unfolds encompassing the Cascade and Olympic Mountain Ranges, Mount Rainier, Puget Sound, Lake Union, and, of course, the city itself. Here too are exhibits that describe the view, area activities, other towers throughout the world, and the construction of the Needle. Directly below the observation deck are two restaurants that make a revolution once each hour. At the 100-foot level, there are three banquet rooms, while, on the plaza level, there are shops featuring clothing, gifts, and crafts of the Pacific Northwest.

Set on a foundation 30 feet deep, the massive structure is built of 147,000 pounds of steel and weighs 3,700 tons. The Needle has been closed only twice for safety reasons, during storms with winds of more than 75 miles an hour.

At its base is Seattle Center, an extensive complex that includes the Pacific Science Center, the International Fountain, an amusement park, the city's major performing arts companies, and a monorail linking the parklike setting to the city's downtown.

From the observation deck of the 605-foot Space Needle, one can view a stunning panorama of Seattle and the surrounding area.

Additional Information

The Northeast

Atlantic City, pp. 30–31
Atlantic CityConvention and Visitors Bureau
2314 Pacific Avenue
Atlantic City, New Jersey 08401
(609) 348-7100

Fallingwater, p. 35
P.O. Box R
Mill Run, Pennsylvania 15464
(412) 329-8501

**Ft. McHenry National Monument
& Historic Shrine**, p. 38
National Park Service
East Fort Avenue
Baltimore, Maryland 21230
(301) 962-4290

Freedom Trail, pp. 10–13
Greater Boston Convention & Visitors Bureau
Visitors Information Department
Prudential Plaza
P.O. Box 490
Boston, Massachusetts 02199
(617) 536-4100

Gettysburg National Military Park, pp. 36–37
Gettysburg, Pennsylvania 17325
(717) 334-1124

Harvard University, p. 14
Harvard University Information Center
Holyoke Center
1350 Massachusetts Avenue
Cambridge, Massaachusetts 02138
(617) 495-1573

Hyde Park, p. 18
National Park Service
249 Albany Post Road
Hyde Park, New York 12538
(914) 229-9115

Independence Park, pp. 32–34
Philadelphia Convention & Visitors Bureau
Tourist Information Department
1515 Market Street, Suite 2020
Philadelphia, Pennsylvania 19102
(215) 636-1666

Niagara Falls

Inner Harbor, p. 39
Harborplace and the Gallery
200 E. Pratt Street
Baltimore, Maryland 21202
(301) 332-4191

Manhattan, pp. 22–27
New York Convention & Visitors Bureau
2 Columbus Circle
New York, New York 10019
(212) 397-8222

The Metropolitan Museum of Art, pp. 28–29
Fifth Avenue & 82nd Street
New York, New York 10028
(212) 535-7710

Niagara Falls, pp. 16–17
Niagara Falls Convention & Civic Center
305 Fourth Street
P.O. Box 1018
Niagara Falls, New York 14302
(716) 286-4769

Plymouth Rock, p. 15
Plymouth County Regional Tourist Council
P.O. Box 1620
Pembroke, Massachusetts 02359
(617) 826-3136

The Statue of Liberty National Monument,
pp. 20–21
Liberty Island
New York, New York 10004
(212) 363-3267

West Point, p. 19
West Point Military Academy Visitors Center
West Point, New York 10996-1788
(914) 938-2638

The Southeast

Arlington National Cemetery, pp. 52–53
Arlington, Virginia 22211
(703) 697-5187

The Biltmore Estate, p. 70
1 North Pack Square
Asheville, North Carolina 28801
(704) 255-1776

Busch Gardens, The Dark Continent,
pp. 78–79
P.O. Box 9158
Tampa, Florida 33764
(813) 988-5171

Busch Gardens, The Old Country, pp. 64–65
P.O. Drawer F-C
Williamsburg, Virginia 23187
(804) 253-3000

Churchill Downs, p. 66
700 Central Avenue
Louisville, Kentucky 40208
(502) 636-3541

Colonial Williamsburg, pp. 58–63
P.O. Box B
Williamsburg, Virginia 23187
(800) H-I-S-T-O-R-Y (toll free)

Walt Disney World, pp. 72–77
Guest Letter
P.O. Box 10000
Lake Buena Vista, Florida 32830
(407) 824-4321

Busch Gardens, The Dark Continent

Everglades National Park, pp. 80–81
P.O. Box 279
Homestead, Florida 33030
(305) 247-6211

Graceland, p. 67
3734 Elvis Presley Blvd.
Memphis, Tennessee 38186
(800) 238-2000 (toll free)
(901) 332-3322

The Grand Old Opry/Opryland, pp. 68–69
Opryland USA Customer Service
2802 Opryland Drive
Nashville, Tennessee 37214
(615) 889-6611

**John F. Kennedy Space Center's
Spaceport USA**, pp. 82–83
Mail Code TWRS
Kennedy Space Center, Florida 32899
(407) 867-1566

Monticello, pp. 56–57
P.O. Box 316
Charlottesville, Virginia 22902
(804) 295-8181

Mt. Vernon, pp. 54–55
Mt. Vernon Ladies Association
Mt. Vernon, Virginia 22121
(703) 780-2000

The Smithsonian Institution, pp. 48–51
Washington, D.C. 20560
(202) 357-1300

Stone Mountain, p. 71
P.O. Box 778
Stone Mountain, Georgia 30086
(404) 656-3592

Washington, D.C., pp. 42–47
Washington Tourist Information Center
1455 Pennsylvania Avenue N.W.
Washington, D.C. 20004
(202) 789-7000

The Central Region

The Alamo, pp. 114–115
P.O. Box 2599
San Antonio, Texas 78299
(512) 225-1391

The Art Institute of Chicago, pp. 92–93
Michigan Avenue & Adams Street
Chicago, Illinois 60603
(312) 443-3600

The Astrodome, p. 109
The Astrodomain
P.O. Box 288
Houston, Texas 77001
(713) 799-9500

Chicago, pp. 86–89
Chicago Tourism Council
Historic Water Tower
806 N. Michigan Avenue
Chicago, Illinois 60611
(312) 280-5740

**The Henry Ford Museum
& Greenfield Village**, pp. 100–103
20900 Oakwood Boulevard
Dearborn, Michigan 48121
(313) 271-1976

The French Quarter, pp. 104–107
Greater New Orleans Tourist Information Board
1520 Sugar Bowl Drive
New Orleans, Louisiana 70112
(504) 566-5011

The Gateway Arch, p. 96
Jefferson National Expansion Memorial Park
11 N. Fourth Street
St. Louis, Missouri 63103
(314) 425-6012

Gilley's Club, p. 108
4500 Spencer Highway
Pasadena, Texas 77504
(713) 941-7990

Lincoln's Home & Tomb, pp. 94–95
Springfield Convention & Visitors Bureau
109 N. Seventh Street
Springfield, Illinois 62701
(800) 545-7300 (toll free)

Mt. Rushmore Memorial Park, pp. 116–117
Attn: Superintendent
P.O. Box 268
Keystone, South Dakota 57751
(605) 574-2523

The Museum of Science & Industry, pp. 90–91
57th Street & Lake Shore Drive
Chicago, Illinois 60637
(312) 684-1414

The Henry Ford Museum & Greenfield Village

Six Flags Over Texas, pp. 110–113
P.O. Box 191
Arlington, Texas 76010
(817) 640-8900

The Truman Home & Library, p. 97
Harry S. Truman National Historic Site
223 N. Main Street
Independence, Missouri 64050
(816) 254-2720

Mark Twain Home & Museum, pp. 98–99
208 Hill Street
Hannibal, Missouri 63401
(314) 221-9010

The West

Carlsbad Caverns National Park, p. 131
Attn: Superintendent
3225 National Parks Highway
Carlsbad, New Mexico 88220
(505) 785-2232

Disneyland, pp. 144–147
1313 Harbor Boulevard
Anaheim, California 92803
(714) 999-4565

The Grand Canyon, pp. 132–134
The Grand Canyon Chamber of Commerce
P.O. Box 3007
Grand Canyon, Arizona 86023
(602) 638-7888

Hoover Dam, p. 127
Hoover Dam Visitors Services
P.O. Box 299
Boulder City, Nevada 89005
(702) 293-8367

Las Vegas, pp. 125–126
Las Vegas Convention & Visitors Authority
3150 Paradise Road
Las Vegas, Nevada 89109
(702) 733-2323

London Bridge, p. 130
Lake Havasu Area Visitors & Convention Bureau
1930 Mesquite Avenue, Suite 3
Lake Havasu City, Arizona 86403
1 (800) 2HAVASU

Los Angeles, pp. 148–151
Los Angeles Convention & Visitors Bureau
695 South Figueroa Street
Los Angeles, California 90017
(213) 689-8822

Los Angeles County Museum of Art,
pp. 156–157
5905 Wilshire Boulevard
Los Angeles, California 90036
(213) 857-6111

Monument Valley, pp. 128–129
P.O. Box 93
Monument Valley, Utah 84536
(801) 727-3287

The Mormon Tabernacle, p. 124
The Church of Jesus Christ of Latter-Day Saints
Public Communications Department
50 E. North Temple Street
Salt Lake City, Utah 84150
(801) 240-2205

The Painted Desert & the Petrified Forest,
pp. 135–137
Petrified Forest National Park
P.O. Box 217
Petrified Forest National Park, Arizona 86028
(602) 524-6228

The Queen Mary & the Spruce Goose,
pp. 142–143
The Queen Mary & the Spruce Goose
Entertainment Center
P.O. Box 8
Long Beach, California 90801
(213) 435-3511

San Diego Zoo, pp. 138–139
P.O. Box 551
San Diego, California 92112
(619) 234-3154

Hoover Dam

San Francisco, pp. 166–171
San Francisco Visitor Information Center
P.O. Box 6977
San Francisco, California 94101
(415) 391-2000

San Simeon State Historical Monument,
pp. 162–165
P.O. Box 8
San Simeon, California 93452
(805) 927-2020 (information)
(619) 452-5956 (reservations)

Sea World, pp. 140–141
1720 South Shores Road
Mission Bay
San Diego, California 92109
(619) 222-6363

The Space Needle, pp. 172–173
203 Sixth Avenue North
Seattle, Washington 98109
(206) 443-9700

Universal Studios Hollywood, pp. 152–155
100 Universal City Plaza
Universal City, California 91608
(818) 508-9600

Yellowstone National Park, pp. 120–123
P.O. Box 168
Yellowstone National Park, Wyoming 82190
(307) 344-7381

Yosemite National Park, pp. 158–161
P.O. Box 577
Yosemite, California 95389
(209) 372-0264

Photo Credits

The Biltmore Co./Biltmore Estate 70

Busch Gardens, The Dark Continent 78, 79, 174 (top)

Busch Gardens, The Old Country 5 (upper right), 64, 65

The Church of Jesus Christ of Latter Day Saints 124 (bottom)

The Colonial Williamsburg Foundation, Williamsburg, VA 58–59

Henry Ford Museum & Greenfield Village 100–01, 103 (top), 175 (bottom)

Four By Five front cover, 2–3, 9–10, 12, 20–21, 21, 22–23, 24, 25, 26–27, 28 (top), 32, 34, 42, 43, 44–45, 47 (top), 52 (right), 56 (top), 57, 66, 67 (top), 71, 72–73, 74–75, 76, 77, 83, 84–85, 88 (right), 93, 96, 116–17, 120, 121, 126, 132–33, 144–45, 146–47, 148, 149, 151, 164–65, 170, 172–173, back cover

Gilley's 108

Houston Sports Association 109

Los Angeles County Museum of Art 156, 157

Louisiana Office of Tourism 107 (top)

Maryland Tourism Office 39

Missouri Division of Tourism 97 (bottom)

The Museum of Science of Industry 90

The National Air & Space Museum, Smithsonian Institution 50 (top)

The National Museum of American History, Smithsonian Institution 50 (bottom)

New York State Dept. of Economic Development 19 (bottom), 174 (bottom)

Opryland U.S.A., Inc. 68, 69 (top)

Pennsylvania Bureau of Tourism 5 (upper left)

Philadelphia Convention & Visitors Bureau 33

The Queen Mary & Spruce Goose Entertainment Center 142, 143

Sea World Inc. 140, 141

Six Flags Over Texas 110, 111, 112, 112–113

Smithsonian Institution, Office of Architectural History & Historic Preservation 51

Vic Stiles 130

SuperStock International 6, 10–11, 13, 14, 15, 16, 16–17, 18, 19 (top), 27, 28, 29, 30–31, 35 (top), 36–37, 37, 38, 40–41, 41, 46, 47, 48–49, 52 (left), 53, 54, 55, 56 (bottom),60–61, 61, 62, 75, 82–83, 86, 87, 88 (left), 89, 91, 92, 94 (top), 95, 98, 99, 102, 103, 104–105, 106, 107 (bottom), 117, 122–23, 124 (left), 125, 127, 128–29, 134, 135, 136–37, 145, 150, 158–59, 160, 161, 162, 163, 166, 167, 168, 169, 171

Tennessee Tourist Authority 67 (bottom), 69 (bottom)

Texas Dept. of Commerce, Tourism Division 5 (lower left) 114–15

The Truman Home 97 (top)

The U.S. Bureau of Reclamation 175 (top)

U.S. Dept. of the Interior, National Park Service 44, 80–81, 81, 94 (bottom), 131

Universal City Studios 152, 154–55

Virginia Division of Tourism 63, 176

Western Pennsylvania Conservancy 35 (bottom)

Wyoming Travel Commission 5 (lower right)

Zoological Society of San Diego 138, 139

Acknowledgments

We gratefully thank the following for their assistance in making possible the publication of *American Landmarks and Popular Places*:

The Astrodomain, Ethan Cartwright; Atlantic City Convention & Visitors Bureau, Cindy Clagett; Biltmore Estate, Travis P. Leaford; Carlsbad Caverns — U.S. Dept. of the Interior/ National Park Service, Bob Crisman; The Church of Jesus Christ of Latter-Day Saints, Don LeFevre; Colonial Williamsburg, Norm Beatty; Commonwealth of Kentucky Dept. of Travel Development, Fred Curtis; Congregational Library, Harold F. Worthley; Dept. of Parks & Recreation — San Simeon Region, John Blades; Fallingwater, Linda Wagner; Fleishman Hillard, Inc., Jayne Bloch; Florida Dept. of Commerce, Dixie Nimms; Henry Ford Museum & Greenfield Village, Lori Dick; Gilley's, Leo Beck; Graceland, Meredith Phillips; Harvard University, Margery Heffron; Hearst San Simeon State Historical Monument, Sally Scott and Rick Johnson; Hermitage, Edith Thornton; Inner Harbor, Liz Englewitz; J.F. Kennedy Space Center, Jo Murphy; Kentucky Derby, Dick Duncan; Las Vegas News Bureau/Las Vegas Convention Center, Milt Palmer; London Bridge, Wendy Martinson & Vic Stiles; Los Angeles County Museum of Art, Pamela Jenkins; Jean Luther and Assoc., Laurie Dominic; Macy's Public Relations, Sean Sullivan; Monticello, Millie Travis; Mount Vernon, Barbara MacMillan & Karen Peters; Museum of Science and Industry, Nancy Hart; National Air & Space Museum — Smithsonian Institution, Joyce Peterson; National Museum of American History — Smithsonian Institution, Kate Henderson; Neiman Marcus, Pat Zajak; New York State Dept. of Economic Development, John C. Cusano; New Jersey Dept. of Commerce, Energy & Economic Development, Jean D. McDougall; Old South Church, Jean Howard; Opryland USA, Inc., Judy Mizell; Philadelphia Convention & Visitors Bureau, Susan Oates; Pike's Peak, Debbie Kovalik; The Queen Mary & Spruce Goose Entertainment Center, Richard Kerlin & Jennifer Nestegard; Quinn Brien, Inc., Helen Williford; Renaissance Center, Diana MacLean; The Paul Revere Memorial Association, Michael A. McBride; Franklin D. Roosevelt Home — Hyde Park, George Bearndt; San Diego Zoo, Laurie Krusinski; Sears Tower, Kathy Gucfa; Six Flags Over Texas, Bruce Neal & Shari Rose; Smithsonian Institution, Joyce Goulait, Tanya Garner, & Carrie R. Harrison; Smithsonian Institution — Office of Architectural History & Historic Preservation, Cynthia Field; South Dakota Dept. of Tourism, Mark Kayser; State of Louisiana Dept. of Culture, Recreation & Tourism, Al Godoy, & Sharon Johnson; Tennessee Tourist Development Office, Carlynne Foster; Texas Dept. of Commerce, Richard Reynolds; Truman Home National Historic Site, Palma Wilson-Buell & Steven D. Harrison; Harry S Truman Library, George H. Curtis; Mark Twain Home & Museum, Henry Sweets; Universal Studios, Jim Yeager; United Nations, Margaret Riddle; U.S. Bureau of Reclamation — Lower Colorado Region, Tom Hughes; U.S. Dept. of the Interior — National Park Service, Bill Clark & Rosa M. Wilson; West Point Military Academy, Major Ed Evans.

Mount Vernon